Why We Write

Why We Write

THE POLITICS AND PRACTICE OF WRITING
FOR SOCIAL CHANGE

EDITED BY JIM DOWNS

Routledge
Taylor & Francis Group

New York   London

Published in 2006 by
Routledge
Taylor & Francis Group
711 Third Avenue,
New York, NY 10017

Published in Great Britain by
Routledge
Taylor & Francis Group
2 Park Square
Milton Park, Abingdon
Oxon OX14 4RN

International Standard Book Number-10: 0-415-97320-1 (Hardcover) 0-415-97321-X (Softcover)
International Standard Book Number-13: 978-0-415-97320-5 (Hardcover) 978-0-415-97321-2 (Softcover)
Library of Congress Card Number 2005024926

Library of Congress Cataloging-in-Publication Data

Why we write: the politics and practice of writing for social change / edited by Jim Downs.
    p. cm.
  Includes bibliographical references and index.
  ISBN 0-415-97320-1 (hb : alk. paper) -- ISBN 0-415-97321-X (pb : alk. paper)
  1. Authorship--Social aspects. 2. Academic writing--Social aspects. 3. Literature and society. I. Downs, Jim, 1973-

PN145.W46 2006
808'.02--dc22
                                                      2005024926

For G.N.D.
Sagapo Poli

ACKNOWLEDGMENTS

This volume grew out of the Why We Write conference held at Columbia University in the spring of 2003. The conference was the second part of a series of conferences organized by graduate students in the history department that explored issues related to history, social change, and the politics of writing. The proceedings from the first conference were published as *Taking Back the Academy: History of Activism, History as Activism* (Routledge, 2004).

The Why We Write conference drew participants from across disciplines and academic fields and also included, among others, filmmakers, journalists, playwrights, novelists, and poets from in and beyond the United States. The focus of the conference was to examine writing, broadly defined. As such the panels ranged from historical discussions on print culture and the use of theory in U.S. history to roundtable discussions on gender and sexuality to workshops on teaching writing and publishing one's research. Novelist Dorothy Allison delivered the opening keynote address, and the participants included scholars such as Carroll Smith-Rosenberg, Robin Kelley, Elsa Barkley Brown, Gayatri Spivak, Nancy Hewitt, Eve Sedgwick, Susan Sturm, Alice Kessler-Harris, John Demos, Carol Gluck, Susan Brownmiller, Ellie DeLapi, Temma Kaplan, Christine Stansell, Jill Lepore, Jennifer Morgan, Michele Mitchell, John D'Emilio, Catherine Clinton, Ricki Sollinger, Alan Brinkley, Christopher Cappazola, Ashli White, Deb Margolin, Ann Fabian, and Jennifer Manion.

My first and most important debt is to all of these writers and scholars, who took time from their busy schedules and traveled without pay or financial reimbursement to support a graduate student conference. Their participation made the conference a truly remarkable and memorable event for all involved. I am very indebted to the countless writers, scholars, and students who attended the panels and sessions, raising provocative questions, making insightful comments, and compelling the authors in this volume to continue the conversation. No deft turn of phrase can adequately express my gratitude and admiration for those who found the time and energy to turn their essays into printed form. They have not only provided an opportunity for the many who never made it to the conference with a chance to become engaged with the ideas, but they have powerfully demonstrated why we write.

For helping with the organization of the conference, I remain grateful to the history department administration, namely Alan Brinkley and Alice Kessler-Harris for their guidance, assistance, and financial support. Eric Foner has been and continues to be a source of encouragement. His published writings and active involvement in the historical profession have inspired many of his students in more ways than he probably knows. I am extremely grateful to all of the graduate students at Columbia for helping organizing the conference, particularly Nancy Kwak, Elizabeth Herbin, Lisa Ford, Janice Traflet, Caitlin L. Crowell, Lisa Ramos, Theresa Ventura, Ted McCormick, Nick Turse, and Jennifer Fronc. From the start, Jennifer Manion discussed every last detail of conference planning and book editing with me, offering keen insights and advice throughout the process. I am not sure how or even if I would do all of this if she were not such a fundamental part of my life and work.

Kimberly Guinta, my editor at Routledge, has given new meaning to the term patience. Her valuable suggestions and help in the course of compiling this volume as well as her commitment to the ideas presented in it are commendable. Catherine Clinton's support of this project and her help navigating me through the tumultuous and unexpected tides of organizing a conference and then publishing a book are rare, indeed.

Finally, Lynda Hart's writings have inspired me in more ways than I know or even wish to tally. Her influence is inscribed on these pages, as she always knew the power and importance of writing for change.

CONTENTS

INTRODUCTION: WHEN AND WHY WE ENTER

Jim Downs

A novelty greeting card depicts an office filled with books stacked on the floor, brimming on the shelves, and piled on all the chairs. Inside the card, the inscription reads, "Too bad academics don't get writer's block." The physical representation of the countless books overtaking the room indicts scholarly production, while the humor derives from the cultural attitude that academic books are useless. According to the card, academic books are overabundant, and scholarship is—to borrow another cultural cliché—isolated in an "ivory tower."

It is easy to criticize the nonacademic world for not taking scholarship seriously or understanding its purpose. And it is even easier to ignore such a card and chalk it up to another example of the "closing of the American mind." It is more difficult, however, to acknowledge its truth and recognize it as a warning. Once we do—once we allow such a sentiment to bounce around the corners of our minds—we can't help but ask, Why? Why do academics write? With the thousands of articles, books, dissertations, book reviews, essays, volumes, anthologies, and textbooks published each year, many of which will only be read by handfuls of people, why do academics continue to write? Certainly part of the answer to this question lies in the cliché "publish or perish." At the starting point of their careers, most academics did not have a fear of perishing, but rather were sparked by an inspiration to write. "Publish or perish" serves as a resigning retort in response to the anguish of writing, the search for the right topic, the right word, which is then followed by the search for a publisher, and the hassle of rechecking footnotes and compiling indexes—not to mention the all-too-familiar daily

1

problems of laptops breaking down, printers jamming, and computer files mysteriously disappearing.

The objective of this volume is to move beyond the many challenging and debilitating frustrations endured by those of us who live by their pens, and to return to the place or the moment that inspired us to write in the first place. Before we outline our next article or even author another book review, we need to spend more time thinking about the larger motivations for writing and publishing. While academics often divide themselves by discipline, geography, and period, raising questions about why we write pertains to all of us, regardless of field or specialty. As such, this volume brings together a number of academics from fields as diverse as history, nursing, women's studies, and law in order to think collectively about the larger aims of scholarly production, providing an ideal opportunity for interdisciplinary collaboration.

Emphasizing the process of writing and asking ourselves why and even how we write responds to the cultural criticism that views scholarly writing as useless, and it instead allows us to reflect on the larger issues of scholarly production more generally. Consequently, the essays in this book represent wide-ranging and diverse perspectives on the process of academic writing. Moving beyond the monograph, this book explores the personal and political motivations for writing, while at the same time probing the process and approaches to writing scholarship. The objective here is to not only to offer insights into why we write but also to consider the theoretical and methodological questions of how we write. Because many scholars' attempts to challenge or refute traditional interpretations derive from formulating new theories or creating new models of interpretation, the subject of how we write is intimately tied to questions of why we write.

* * *

Section I, "Why I Write: Personal Reflections" includes personal accounts by established scholars explaining their motivation and objectives in writing. Through accounts that detail how the political climate of the 1960s and 1970s influenced their decision to become scholars to personal stories of how they envision their work within the classroom and literary marketplace, these scholars offer insightful and provocative narratives on the place of scholarship in the twenty-first century. The goal of this section is not only to learn about these authors' lives and to see the connection between their personal goals and intellectual work but also to foster a conversation among scholars about how they envision and understand their scholarship. By not offering a place or opportunity for such reflection, scholarship risks being locked off in an ivory tower or viewed only as a means for professional advancement.

The authors included in this section represent an exciting cast of scholars. They each became historians for different reasons, and practice the craft differently. Despite their differences in approach, their essays collectively reveal the ways in which they challenged mainstream understandings of U.S. history and how the political climate in which they wrote greatly influenced their choice of topic. Energized by the emergence of gay liberation in New York City in the 1970s, John D'Emilio describes his experience as a graduate student and his decision to become a historian, while Catherine Clinton recounts her experience as a young scholar in the 1980s and her contribution to the then growing field of women's history. After a discussion of life in graduate school, D'Emilio provides a brief overview of his later work and its connection to larger political issues. Clinton's essay departs from an overtly political narrative, and chronicles her work in reaching out to the public by writing children's books and popular history texts while still maintaining a commitment to write history that encompasses the experience of those typically marginalized in U.S. history. Both Clinton's and D'Emilio's chapters offer a rare glimpse into the struggles and politics that surrounded their deeply personal decisions to re-tell American history.

As a graduate student in the late 1990s, Timothy Patrick McCarthy read books by Clinton, D'Emilio, and other scholars/activists committed to challenging traditional interpretations of American history. Inspired by these authors and their books, McCarthy as a young graduate student in New York became actively involved in the political issues then seething on college campuses. For McCarthy, scholarship was not divorced from his activist interests but was intricately connected. In his essay, McCarthy charts his experience as a scholar/activist and reflects on the critical ways that intellectuals can respond—both in out and out of the classroom—to current political and social issues.

Working as a community organizer in Boston in the late 1980s, Jennifer Morgan began to yearn for "subtle identity politics" to "theorize the boundaries of identity," which circumscribed her political engagement. She decided to enroll in graduate school at Duke University to become a historian since she had "faith in the transformative power of narrative." Fascinated by the women she read about in the North Carolina state archives, Morgan set out to tell their story. But the historical writing of enslaved women in the colonial United States was complicated, and as Morgan explains in her essay, researching the lives of enslaved women called into question the creation and organization of archives as well as the politics of identity. In her essay, Morgan reveals that writing against a historiography that barely acknowledged the experience of bondswomen in the 1700s meant reevaluating historical evidence and the process by which historians read and interpret sources.

Taking their cue from Morgan's investigation of how we write history, the authors in section II, "The Process of Writing," explore new and innovative approaches to answering complicated historical questions. From concerns about how to write transnational history to addressing polemics concerning the discovery of sexual violence in the past, these scholars detail their research questions and experiences in order to begin a much-needed conversation about the process of historical writing.

Too often today, historians call for new models of analysis but seldom offer a reflection or a proscription on how to actually adopt such approaches in historical writing. This section of the book responds to this problem by offering an opportunity for scholars to reflect on the process of writing history and to consider how one evaluates evidences, constructs archives, and, ultimately, writes history. As questions of foreign policy, for instance, continue to inform public debate, historians' research into the history of foreign relations has intensified. Under the banner of "transnationalism," historians have raised questions about the past that transcend the traditional writing of national history. Questioning and researching U.S. involvement abroad in issues related to imperialism, trade, and even religion, these historians have not simply compared and contrasted difference between nations; instead, as historian David Thelan explained in the *Journal of American History*,

> We wanted to explore how people and ideas and institutions and cultures moved above, below, through, and around, as well as within, the nation-state, to investigate how well national borders contained or explained how people experienced history. We wanted to observe how people, moving through time and space according to rhythms and relationships of their own, drew from, ignored, constructed, transformed, and defied claims of the nation-state.[2]

Yet the question remains, How? Jung H. Pak attempts to answer this question or, at the very least, to reveal the problems and struggles one faces when one actually attempts to write transnational history. For her doctoral dissertation, Pak wanted to tell the story of how many sons and daughters of American missionaries eventually became involved in U.S. public policy, but in order to tell that story Pak needed to move to Korea to conduct her research. Trained as a U.S. historian, Pak explains in her essay how she struggled to adjust to a different system of archival organization, improve her language skills, and had to ultimately rise above gendered stereotypes that questioned her integrity as a scholar. While Pak considers transitional history a worthwhile intellectual and academic endeavor, her essay raises many questions for scholars to consider in writing history across national boundaries.

In addition to the emergence of transnational history, studies of gender and sexuality have produced significant retellings of the past in the last twenty years or so. In her essay, Jennifer Fronc discusses her first encounter—while conducting research in the New York Public Library archives—with a collection of sources that described forced sexual encounter as told by male progressive reformers, and explains her uncertainty on how to evaluate such records. Aware of the explosive feminist debates on the subject of rape, Fronc focuses her essay on the narrative construction of rape as it is circumscribed by the language of forced sexual encounter, violence, and desire in twentieth-century municipal documents. She asks many provocative and unsettling questions on how to write about these sources, and in so doing, raises larger questions about how to write about the history of sexuality.

Further exploring how to write the history of sexuality, Caitlin Love Crowell broadens our understanding of sexual experience by raising questions about the history of intimacy. In her essay, Crowell considers the intimate life of the late-nineteenth-century activist, scholar, and educator Anna Julia Cooper. Crowell not only explores a neglected area of historical inquiry, but her essay beautifully meditates on the process and politics of writing about how love and sexuality shaped the lives of those in the past.

Moving from the private sphere to the public sphere, Jill Lepore considers larger questions about the place of history in mainstream culture. The recent explosion of what Lepore defines as "history for profit"—namely, blockbuster biographies, television's History Channel, and historical epics—has stirred controversy among historians who have been ambitiously attempting to correct the public's nostalgic understanding of the past. Framing her analysis around historian Sean Wilentz's statement that "'American history was meant to rattle its readers, not to confirm them in their received myths and platitudes about America,'" Lepore explores the growing phenomenon of the history craze among contemporary readers and thoughtfully contemplates its meaning for historians in the twenty-first century. Her essay offers an opportunity for scholars to reflect on the ways in which their research and the politics of their research intersect with larger cultural currents.

As history—according to Lepore—continues to remain "hot," Drew Faust explores historians and the public's fascination with the subject of war. In her contribution to the volume, Faust focuses on the connection between historians of the Civil War and the actual actors who fought in the battles. Historians, Faust explains, have been intoxicated by the war; but this intoxication, she notes, can be traced to Union and Confederate soldiers themselves, who cautioned that they "may grow too fond" of the war. Tracing the recent fascination among historians and U.S. audiences with studying the Civil War, Faust offers a rich and original exploration of why we write and read about war.

Recognizing the links between the past and present, the authors in section III, "The Politics of Writing," consider the ways that writing can be used in the service of social change. For these authors, documenting their personal experience is crucial to their political mission. From recounting strictly autobiographical narratives to analyzing how writing and scholarship can lead to a just world, the contributors to this section dare readers to move beyond the walls of the academy to consider the value and use of their scholarship.

Miles away from their cozy offices and the comfort of their classroom routines, Eleanor M. Novek and Rebecca Sanford enter a women's correctional facility in New Jersey to teach inmates on a daily basis. Trained in the social sciences, Novek and Sanford use their academic credentials to work with and support women in prison. In their essay, Novek and Sanford explain how teaching the women writing skills provides the inmates with a powerful mode of expression. Novek and Sanford's essay reveals how the inmates—by reaching back into their own history and expressing their concerns, frustrations, and aspirations—found writing a way to save their lives. The essay not only sheds light on the many possible opportunities for scholars to use their academic tools in the form of social change far from the walls of academe but imparts a poignant message about the power of autobiography.

Free from disciplinary constraints and academic jargon, autobiography as a genre gets at the crux of why we write. Like the women in prison who experienced the power of writing through the process of telling their own stories, Sasha Kamini Parmasad, in her essay, chronicles her desire to write. Unlike the other authors in the volume, Parmasad is not trained in the social sciences or humanities, but instead is—as she describes herself—an "amateur hungry writer." Her piece points to the power of autobiography to stretch our conceptions of the intersections between memoir and history, past and present and, most of all, between the desire to write and the politics of social change. Meditating on her personal history as a descendent of Indian indentured laborers in Trinidad, Parmasad illustrates how autobiographies disrupt traditional interpretations of the past and lend a more human perspective to the social and political transformations that too often dominate historical narration.

Further demonstrating the way that personal experiences shape and even haunt why we write, Jodi Bromberg's own experience as a law student inspires her critique of legal training and the construction of the legal academy. A political activist, Bromberg laments the lack of opportunity within legal education to create social change. Claiming that law school, like most professional graduate programs, indoctrinates students into accepting the "status quo," Bromberg uses her personal saga as a social activist in law school to expose the limitations and political problems that stifle initiatives for social change in the legal academy.

Building on the politics of writing for social change, Daniel J. Sherman, a political scientist, raises critical questions about conducting fieldwork and the importance of his scholarship to the communities in which he studies. Curious about how particular communities mobilized in response to radioactive waste in their backyards, Sherman set out to study the various ways in which each community responded to these environmental crises, but in the course of his research he began developing relationships with the subjects of study—which redirected his approach to the work. Sherman's essay offers an important reflection on the decisions that researchers and writers must make in their attempts to balance their scholarly obligations with their broader political commitment for social change.

So committed to social action that she doesn't have time to write, the final contributor to the volume exclaims, "Why I don't write." While so much of this book testifies to the value of writing in creating change and illuminating connections between the past and the present, Erme C. Maula, a Ph.D. candidate in nursing, is just plain exhausted. Self-described as the "advocate's advocate," Maula points to the problems and struggles of activists that actually use writing as a form of social change. Her essay raises important questions about an otherwise neglected area of social change discourse: the inability to write, and the time and finances needed to do so. In spite of these challenges, Maula's essay articulates many of the major themes in the book. It shows how a professional field such as nursing needs writers and historians to record the concerns of those in the profession; it alludes to historical issues that shape current social activist agendas; and it reveals the autobiographical impulses that inspire us to imagine a better future, to witness the connections between past and present, and, ultimately, to write.

Section I

Why I Write: Personal Reflections

1

WHY I WRITE

John D'Emilio

One can never predict what a simple invitation to write an essay or give a talk can provoke. Thinking about this book and the theme of the conference that inspired it has made me realize how lucky I am and how blessed I have been. I have had a solid quarter century of writing of things that I care about passionately and that at least a few other folks care about, too. Every day I carry with me the certainty that the heart of my work, my writing, has made a difference in the world.

Why do I write? I write because someone—a fellow graduate student—told me one day that I was good at it. More than three decades later, I remember the moment as if it happened yesterday. A small group of Columbia University history students were meeting at my Riverside Drive railroad flat to put together the next issue of *Common Sense*, our rabble-rousing newsletter. Except for my desk, which was a six-foot-long plank stretched across a pair of two-drawer file cabinets, everything else was close to the ground. My bed was on the floor. My dining table was a painted wood board resting on milk crates. My sofa was the mattress of a twin bed pressed against a wall with some pillows as backing and a paisley-patterned sheet as covering. Several of us were squatting on the floor and hunched over the table, rulers in hand, painstakingly creating headlines by pressing letters, one at a time, onto the mock-up of our newsletter. Richard, meanwhile, had wandered over to my desk where he stood reading pages of my not-yet-proofed master's essay. He looked down in my direction and, with a mixture of surprise and admiration, said, "You write so well!"

Richard and I had only a passing acquaintance. He was a year ahead of me in the program; he had no reason at all to flatter me. No one had ever said such a thing to me before, and it was shocking and revelatory. It opened up for me the possibility that writing—not simply research, study, or teaching—was something I might do.

Why else do I write? I write because reading history books saved my life, and I have been bold—or foolish—enough to think that maybe my writing could do the same for someone else.

The northeast Bronx, where I grew up, was more than a world away from the Morningside Heights campus of Columbia. The combination of fervid anticommunism and Roman Catholic moral absolutism made for an environment in which certitude was a fundamental principle. The description of God in the Baltimore catechism ("He always was, always will be, and always remains the same") extended to every aspect of life ("it always was this way, always will be this way, and always remains this same way"). This was not a comforting worldview for a boy on the edge of adolescence with his first inklings of an unorthodox sexuality.

One of the main ways I dealt with this discomfort was by getting lost in books. Many of those books were novels filled with characters whose lives were thoroughly unlike anything I knew. Heroic courage, undying passion, bottomless grief: the emotions and the experiences took me beyond the dulling sameness of everyday life. But novels were make-believe. They were engines of pleasure that, in the end, didn't count for much in the hardnosed practical world of my youth. History by contrast was real. It happened. It mattered. The lesson I took from the history books I read (not the social history of ordinary people and popular insurgencies, but narratives of royalty, empire, generals, and war) was that change is the essence of life. What once was will not be again; nothing ever remains the same. The comfort I extracted from this was indescribably sweet. I wanted to tell it to the world.

But these are not the only, and perhaps not even the main, reasons why I write. Most of all I write because my life intersected with a vibrant social movement that made writing a powerful, vivid, and compelling activity. At the time this intersection seemed serendipitous, almost accidental. Later it came to seem overdetermined: how could a young gay man shaped by the student protests and antiwar activism of the late 1960s, sporting the long hair, beard, and sandals of the counterculture and living in New York City, not be swept up by the drama of gay liberation? Later still I came to view my involvement as far more intentional on my part. After all, I chose my friendships, made decisions about how to spend my time, returned again and again to meetings, conferences and demonstrations, and came out in settings that helped guide me along particular paths.

My impulse to write the kind of history that I do had almost no connection to professional aspiration or ambition. My imagined audience wasn't then, and still hasn't become, the academy or the world of formally trained historians. In the 1970s to write gay history and to have a career as an academic historian seemed self-evidently mutually exclusive. These two activities were so incompatible that to choose gay history as my subject matter meant that I simultaneously searched for a public other than university students and professional scholars.

That public was coming to life in the 1970s. It was small in numbers, yet it also had a discernible social weight to it. And it was growing.

The gay male world of the 1970s was different both from what came before and what exists today in large urban centers. I remember gay bars in New York City during the late 1960s. Heavy doors and darkened windows protected patrons from any peering eyes outside. These were nighttime places, free from at least some of the dangers that socializing in daylight might have posed. Just a few years later, everything seemed new and uncontainably exuberant. Crowds of men spilled out of bars, milled around on the sidewalk with an utter lack of concern about what the police might do, and brazenly cruised the streets of Greenwich Village.

Exciting as this new world was, it sometimes appeared desperately fragile, even rootless. Many of the men populating these bars led vibrantly queer social lives even as almost no one who was straight knew that they were gay. They stood uncertainly poised on the threshold of the closet door. Around them, in the bars, on the streets, in the pages of a new queer press that was distributed on newsstands and handed out in bars, a smaller number of men was propagating a new ethic of coming out, of self-revelation, of unabashedly wearing one's gayness everywhere.

In those years, queer activism was easier to fall into than it is today. It seemed natural, as much a way of being as a set of activities. It had not yet been professionalized into full-time paying jobs that only a few community members held. Nor was it neatly compartmentalized under the rubric of middle-class volunteerism, a few hours spent each week or month with an organization that served the community. Instead, it could be expressed on the spot by responding to one of the many flyers that circulated all the time, announcing a rally or a march. It displayed itself through the conversations one chose to initiate among straight friends and coworkers, or the proselytizing about coming out that one did at bars, in bathhouses, or on the streets in the course of one's own socializing. It took form for me in part through the reorientation of my work life. More and more of my time was spent contributing, in effect, to movement building and social change in ways that felt almost effortless.

Gay stuff hadn't come to saturate mass culture, the media, and the arts as it has now. Gay also hadn't yet gone glossy, with the pages of our publications imitating *People* and other worshipers of celebrity ("42 Music Stars on Gay Marriage"—shouts the cover of an issue of the *Advocate* that lies in my study—"We're for It!"). Instead, the queer community of those years sustained a set of publications that were oppositional. Some of them had wonderful names like *Fag Rag*, *Sinister Wisdom*, *Gay Sunshine*, and *Amazon Quarterly*. Their cheap newsprint made them ephemeral and, hence, all the more precious. They were produced by staffs who weren't paid and their pages were filled by writers who weren't compensated. Circulations were in the thousands. They were among the few places where gay men and lesbians could find reflected back to us the stance of pride that we were trying to project into the community and the culture at large. They were looking for material to print that had substance and that was accessible.

Writing gay history seemed a way to participate in making this new world. In a decade when Alex Haley's book *Roots* and the television series made from it sparked a national preoccupation with finding and claiming one's cultural antecedents, history tapped especially powerful emotions in gay men and lesbians, few of whom had come of age with any sense of a past that was about them. History filled a hunger, an aching need.

This emergent community made spaces for these newly uncovered stories about the past. Almost all of the first histories to make it into print, books like Jonathan Ned Katz's *Gay American History*, John Boswell's *Christianity, Social Tolerance, and Homosexuality*, and my own *Sexual Politics, Sexual Communities*, were rehearsed as performances or lectures or classes for community audiences before taking publishable form. In a number of cities, local community-based history projects dug up documents, artifacts, and images, and their members combined these into slide talks, films, panel discussions, and books. Periodicals like the ones mentioned above, as well as the *Body Politic* out of Toronto and the *Gay Community News* from Boston, opened their pages to accessibly written pieces about the gay, lesbian, and transgender past. A writer could see his or her words translated very quickly into action, wielded as a tool for building new lives and communities. It was a great motivation for writing and, for me, it made writing a passionate pursuit.

When I think about the large projects that have consumed me over the years—projects that have fed into, or been fed by, smaller ones—they have all been firmly situated in a present moment that compelled me to look at the past and write about it. I was drawn to what became *Sexual Politics, Sexual Communities* in order to offer a more capacious historical tradition to those of us who were gay liberationists in the 1970s and who often felt as if our activism had no antecedents. I wrote *Intimate Matters* with Estelle Freedman in the 1980s because of the fierce sexuality debates that were fracturing feminism, because of the reactionary conservatism of the administration of Ronald Reagan and its impact on sexual politics, and because of the urgent need to think expansively about sex in the context of the first years of the AIDS epidemic. I have fed and deepened my thinking and writing about social movements and the politics of sexuality by long immersions in the kind of worlds that I write about. Over the years, this sort of reciprocity has kept me wanting to write.

The book that I have just finished—a biography of Bayard Rustin, a Gandhian activist, radical pacifist, and civil rights strategist—has absorbed me for a dozen years. It is bigger, measured by numbers of pages, than anything I've written before. The motives that drew me to Rustin's life were more complicated than those that sparked other projects. The push to write about him came from the emotional residues still lingering from my time as an undergraduate in Morningside Heights in the late 1960s; it came from experiences in the classroom with undergraduates who wanted explanations and insights about the 1960s that I didn't have; and it rose out of the dilemmas that I saw queer activists confronting at the height of AIDS politics in the early 1990s. Without my intending it, the work on Rustin has been framed by the two Gulf Wars. I began the project the month after the first one started, and I finished the book the month before this most recent one began.

The issues that Rustin's life puts before us have never seemed more compelling to address. He believed that war would never bring peace, and violence would never bring justice. He saw nationalism as a destructive force in human affairs. He believed that economic insecurity and inequality made a sham out of political democracy. When I ask myself why I write in the context of this book I've just finished—in the midst of this war my government is waging, in a political moment as repellent as any I've experienced in my lifetime, when our national government's devotion to no one but the rich and powerful isn't even masked—I also ask myself, How do I make use of these words?

I imagine spending the next couple of years on the road with Bayard Rustin. I see myself taking him, or at least my account of his life, to a range of venues: to bookstores, community centers, and university lecture halls; radio talk shows and webpages; newspapers, magazines, and organizational newsletters. I want to use this writing as an opportunity to create spaces, real and virtual, in which audiences can coalesce and conversations can occur, so that together folks can reflect about issues of war and peace, racial and economic justice, and forms of democracy that are both local and global.

As I plot these activities, I realize that the reason I have continued to write is because it's the way that I've found to keep issues like this at the center of my life.

2

WHY I WRITE

Catherine Clinton

Those of us who earn our living by publishing, those of us whose mort-gages and children's tuitions depend on advances and royalties, rarely take time for introspection; we are too busy with deadlines and rewrites. We don't have the time for musings and meditations, but I convinced myself a short period of reflection might recharge my batter-ies, which is why I accepted the invitation to participate in first, a conference, and then, a volume with the tantalizing title *Why We Write*.

When I made the decision to go to graduate school in the early 1970s, I was influenced by the fact that I had won a traveling fellowship from Radcliffe College to complete my master's degree in American studies abroad: someone would actually *pay* me to read and write and live in England for a year.[1] I could support myself until I found out whatever it was I wanted to do with my life. It seemed serendipitous that I would dive head first into that bracing comeuppance known as postgraduate training, just as the academy was caving into pressures concerning sex discrimination. Many places decided that instead of thinking up more creative ways to exclude women it was easier just to admit a few.[2] And there I was, application and optimism in hand.

Certainly many go on to graduate studies for lack of imagination, but many more plunge ahead with very specific scenarios in mind, with hopes our writing will be bedazzling or besmirching. But at least *what* we write will have distinctive personal impact, as we add a string of letters to our names—the Ph.D. signaling that at least we finished a magnum opus!

Many of us sally forth with illusions that our scholarship can make a real difference in the world. Our pursuit of academic disciplines is often self-deluding prophecy, but the hothouse of the academy rewards such thinking.

Who among us has not at one time or another, but especially in that first flush of commitment, felt our life being transformed by the power of a book? And the impact of that special book, and perhaps even its author, convinces us to slip into the warm bath of adoration. (Not noticing when the temperature in graduate school is slowly turned up to a boil. . . .)

When I landed in a doctoral program in history in 1975, hard lessons were introduced my first few weeks. What I could or could not write was beside the point; I was there to learn proper deference and behavioral modification to prevent my head from being chopped off by the cruel stroke of defunding.

The most important lesson that my British training had failed to impress upon me was, leave your sense of humor at the door. During the initial meeting of a historical methodology seminar, one young woman, when queried what journals she read regularly, replied with admirable cheek, "*Ladies Home.*" Need I add she didn't last long at my institution, where the ivy was poisonous for those deemed unsuitable. Many women, more than men, had graduate careers that were nasty, brutish, and short.[3]

Once the hazing was over and you made it through to "showtime" (the thesis), waking hours were consumed with writing. What we wrote would define our careers. This is a very daunting prospect for anyone, but especially overambitious twenty-somethings crowded onto competitive campuses. I remember wondering if I should listen to one of my professors who expressed misgivings about my untamed prose: he insisted that I read and heed Ernest Hemingway, although I had already proclaimed allegiance to William Faulkner.

I knew there would be rougher waters ahead when a distinguished scholar, as part of a visiting humanities program, perused my dissertation in progress, a study of the role of the plantation mistress in the half-century following the American Revolution. He told me he was most impressed with my appendix—a statistical study comparing marriage and mortality statistics for Dutch patroons and white Southern planters. I'm sure Hemingway would have been pleased by such a compliment, but fears of what I was getting myself into naturally escalated.

But *why we write* was shifting directions during these formative years. Although I dedicated my energies to an academic career in history, I also looked beyond the academy to think about other ways to display my interests—other venues, besides the scholarly journal, to which I could contribute.

I got my first job in 1979 at a small liberal arts college in upstate New York—becoming the first member of the department to teach women's history, joining my all-male, all-tenured senior colleagues. Despite this academic perch, I decided to keep writing for publication beyond scholarly journals, and to focus on a broader horizon. I do not regret my decision to attempt to write for readers both inside and outside the academy, although it has had its ups and downs.[4]

When I was moving from dissertation to book, I pushed myself beyond the tenure trap. From a very early stage, I always encouraged graduate students to imagine an Aunt Gladys—someone who clearly would read her niece's book out of pride and affection. But why not make it a book that Aunt Gladys would *want* to read—even if her niece hadn't written it? We should all conjure up a theoretical Aunt Gladys, to contemplate a readership beyond a small cadre of scholarly critics. This controversy about our responsibilities to a larger audience has caused heated exchanges and lively disputes within the history profession in recent years.[5]

I was very fortunate to be trained during a time when European scholars such as Fernand Braudel (*Civilization and Capitalism, Fifteenth–Eighteenth Centuries*) and LeRoy Ladruie (*Montaillou*) were not only pioneering exciting approaches to the past, but also redefining audience for historical studies. I knew that something was in the air when one could actually see, as well as imagine, a French medieval "beach read." Was it not a sea change when an academic study—*The Return of Martin Guerre*, by Natalie Davis—became a fabulous film, which then morphed into a Civil War adaptation, *Sommersby* (1993), starring Jodie Foster and Richard Gere? It could be a sea change or just a blip, depending upon a scholarly generation's response to these opportunities.

Yet my Technicolor visions were but a dream in the 1970s, and I had to concentrate on completing a dissertation that would allow me to keep my teaching job. But once the dissertation hurdle was cleared, the book, the publication, the tipping point loomed on the horizon.

Although I had found academic employment, I did not really expect to flourish. I loved the classroom and cherished many of my colleagues, but I had too low a tolerance for academic business as usual—especially in the volatile campus minefields of sexual harassment, pay and promotion equity, maternity leave and child-care policy, and other feminist concerns. These were subjects I found most administrators treated like anthrax: to be contained at all cost. I was gaining a reputation as "Typhoid Mary" for my insistence that policy be set and then enforced. I found the token slot I had was granted with the tacit understanding that I be grateful. But I could not keep up this end of the bargain, nor was I finding it any easier to keep up the role as inside agitator.

I was growing weary of gender battles in my intellectual life, and felt that up close and personal clashes within my teaching institutions were too draining. For example, the chair at my second academic department, where I moved in 1983, suggested that the department he ran was not unlike a monastic order. When I countered that *this* monk was thinking about getting pregnant and required maternity policy guidelines in writing . . . sigh . . . I'll save the rest for my novel.

My commitment to writing provided a crucial crossroads for me at almost every stage of my career. I was struggling to define myself as an academic with my first book, but found my discomfort with academic culture growing. I felt a tension trying to maintain a life outside the academy, then with a husband and hopes for children. As the scholar-monk path lost its appeal, so did the battle to break down prejudice and barriers within the academy.

In addition, after shifting behind the podium with my first academic post, my attitude toward historical writing changed dramatically. I wanted to find books I could teach and discover work that was informative and lively, accessible and smart. And why not write books like these as well? Would that be such a betrayal of my scholarly vows?

Besides Aunt Gladys, there were others who needed good history books, like the first-year student who takes her first history course, one that not only fulfills a requirement but inspires her to read more. The next thing you know, a mind's afire, and whether graduate studies quench or extinguish her enthusiasm we can take pleasure in the ignition, the spark from books that causes us to dream, not put us to sleep.

There are books we read that brim with ideas and insights and show us the way to find our *own* way. These are what started many of us on our path to writing. But how could I become engaged in this kind of historical writing? I needed to concentrate only on research projects, monographs that were meant to make or break an academic future. Yet I decided to take a gamble and plunged into publishing for pay.

The starting salaries for junior faculty were woefully inadequate in the 1980s, especially while paying off graduate school loans. I had to supplement my teaching income at my upstate New York flat by writing. Luckily, I ran into an old college friend who had launched an unusual publishing venture, Story of America—a subscription service of learning American history through topical cards that each bore a glossy image on one side and a 250-word description on the other. Every group of packets came with a bonus triptych, which soon became my specialty: The Making of the Statue of Liberty, Home Life in Colonial America, and the like. My new mission became part of my routine—to take knowledge and research and refine them into simple, direct prose. I would finish on time and for a set fee. This was the secret life of an academic.

But my secret life spilled over into my career. As a result, I not only learned to pull together lectures more painlessly, but I also was able to take on unpaid academic assignments, such as reviews, and to tackle them more effortlessly. Soon I took on and turned in academic reviews on time. My freelance writing paid a bonus, in that supplemental income allowed me to afford a shared sublet in an apartment in New York City.

This writing venture during my earliest years in the academy had personal and professional consequences—I met and married my husband in Manhattan. I learned to enjoy writing, to work hard at it, to struggle toward goals, to see my work in print with a growing sense of accomplishment. Writing under contract convinced me to value my own time and talent—and taught me that others might as well.

I transformed my dissertation into a book—*The Plantation Mistress: Woman's World in the Old South*. Stealing time to read the page proofs on my honeymoon is a memory that evokes ambivalence. But, again, I found myself wedded as well to writing. I did marry someone who had promised, if not to share my obsession, then to tolerate it.[6]

I had learned a thing or two about academic postpartum from observation—"And how is that second book coming? Better this decade than last?" I decided that the cure for a literary letdown, all that anxiety about reviews and related neuroses, would be to start a new project. So I began book number 2 shortly after completing my first manuscript. *Why we write?* To keep a contract in hand, as I have done steadily since I was twenty-seven.

I signed on to write a book for a history series I very much admired, so there I was on my quest, trying to write my second book, *The Other Civil War: American Women in the Nineteenth Century*, while playing beat the clock: I needed to finish my manuscript before my first child was born. And so a new series of complications enters the formula of *why we write* once we produce babies as well as books.

Once my son was born in 1984, and then when my second son arrived in 1989, writing corkscrewed into several different directions for me, as motives and time management spun out of control. I do remember the shock of not caring much about writing the first six months after my first child's birth, as if nursing and composition were incompatible. But it was a great relief to discover that I could fire up the engines and find my way back if I wanted to. That I very much wanted to came as no surprise.

Yet I was finding it increasingly challenging to honor professional commitments, juggling teaching schedules and demanding students while trying to meet family obligations and carve out a reserve of energy for writing. It was particularly disheartening to have to shame women studies' colleagues into creating more flexible schedules—like holding lunchtime talks. I had to protest the standard practice that all guest lectures at four in the afternoon penalized parents of young children, who would have to rush off early to make the day-care pickup. It was a hardscrabble competition to do it all, and plate spinning took an emotional toll. Fear that everything would come tumbling down competed with total exhaustion.

At the same time, writing remained a soothing secret vice—the thing that was my very own. I could cram in a few paragraphs during the wee hours of the morning between feedings. I looked forward to facing my computer after a day of strapping kids in and out of car seats. And, of course, I disappointed many colleagues by letting my personal life dramatically reorder my priorities.

To say the historical profession had become disillusioning to me would be an understatement. In the 1980s and into the 1990s, I had participated in a series of exciting and, in many ways, fulfilling academic projects—including the establishment of women's studies, and at the same time, life support for African-American studies at Harvard University (in the period between the devastating loss of Nathan Huggins and the arrival of Henry Louis Gates, Jr.). But I had also witnessed some dispiriting episodes—many recounted in Jon Wiener's *Historians in Trouble* (2004)—and experienced several personal setbacks climbing the academic ladder. I felt the need to spread my wings.

I became involved in several consulting projects, film collaborations, even textbooks for secondary students; all of these related to my *writing*, and all of these leading away from the feathered nest of academic tenure. My toddlers grew older and articulated their need for and interest in more attention—a time-sensitive demand, as the opposite effect happens as they enter their teens. I knew well that my husband's career deserved the next sacrifice, as he had uprooted his business to move to Boston for my career, and I felt the next move should be his. Thus, forces conspired to convince me to quit teaching full-time. I wanted to try to make my living as a writer.

And so, *why we write* took new twists and shaped my independent resolve during the 1990s. I had often joked with graduate students in the 1980s that instead of trying to publish an article in a prestigious academic journal they should spend less time and aggravation and just write a book. But by the 1990s, I discovered a variety of reasons to complete essays rather than book-length manuscripts. So I began to devote my own energies into shorter pieces, and a good deal of effort into editing what I hoped were smart, compact historical anthologies. This new mission evolved into my own series (*Viewpoints on American Culture*, with Oxford University Press), which provides outlets for a wide range of scholars, but especially emerging academic writers in need of a showcase for their talents and ideas.

Also during this period, I was reading stories to my own children, and became dissatisfied with kid lit offerings. The books for children I encountered seemed disturbingly dated, especially on the topics of race and gender, to which most of my scholarship was dedicated. When will our scholarly innovations and historical discoveries trickle down to the Scholastic Publishing set?

It was a personal as well as professional decision when I gave up working on screenplays in the 1990s to try my hand at children's books. I thought writing children's books would be easier and more satisfying. I was half right.

My books for young readers have been incredibly satisfying, but *easy* is not a word that applies. They are not easy in terms of execution, and difficult to sell. Yet holding these books in my hands, going to a library talk or school visit has offered a remarkable kind of gratification, for which I remain grateful.

The thirty-two-page picture book is as difficult to master as haiku, and remains the gold standard of the trade. At the same time it is a *picture* book, and so your words must inspire the illustrator and, in turn, the reader. I have been lucky thus far in that I have been able to work with illustrators of my choice. I have been very fortunate that these illustrators' extraordinary gifts have made each book a pleasure and a wonder.

When I took on the challenge of doing my first project in this new field—writing history books aimed at ages ten and above—it was extremely daunting. But here was an irresistible gamble for any writer, an opportunity to expand my audience. I was also fortunate in that children's book publishing has become much more sophisticated, with an interest in bringing to children's books the best and brightest new ideas in history. Both historical novels and nonfiction offerings have blossomed in the past decade—and I have met many engaging and enterprising editors with whom to work toward this goal of quality history for young readers. It has been a worthy quest to chase those fickle early readers (and their parents), to try to engage kids' interest in the past.

And after a few encouraging projects, I was willing to become even more adventurous—to write for even younger readers, as I did with my most recent book, *Hold the Flag High*. This is the most humbling and yet most promising reason to write—to inspire someone just beginning to encounter books to understand *why we read*.

We read to expand our worlds; we read to experience a good story; we read to feed and enrich our imaginations. And I think that why some of us *write* is to make this all happen. The more readers we can reach, then the happier we keep our editors (as well as agents and publicists). And, if we don't get lazy, the more we dare to push beyond boundaries.

Some might think we write for acclaim, and I must admit a good review can give a temporary lift. But it's a devil's bargain—if you are going to believe the good reviews, then you need to believe the bad ones as well. I have tried to explain this to writers just starting out. It is equal heresy to novice writers to suggest that prizes and awards are overrated. It defies both what they believe and what they witness.

Literary laurels lift obscure books into the limelight and might gain an author an academic job, a bump in sales, or any number of significant advantages. However, it does not mean that a selected book is qualitatively better because it receives an award. It means the author got lucky.

In my own field of American history, especially, every year people publish terrific work and many prizeworthy books get rewarded. But every year books appear that can change the way people think about specific events, periods, and research fields—even our entire perspective on the past. (And in history it may take several years before the impact of a truly landmark volume makes its mark.) Only a handful of these groundbreaking volumes win awards. Does that mean we should not award prizes—hand out "best" designations and honorable mentions and other professional accolades? No, but if you actually write in hopes that you will receive such an honor, you are likely to be disappointed. And if you earn the sought-after brass ring, you should recognize it as luck—that some prizeworthy books are privileged enough to get prizes while others aren't.

Writing is a secluded occupation and especially difficult for those of us who are gregarious. Book parties, writing groups, and other tricks of the trade do little to alleviate the solitary confinement required. And many a good writer has been ruined by the perpetual lure of lunch.

Especially for scholars, who spend years on campuses enjoying the sense of limitless time for debate and rumination, the discipline required to actually finish writing projects, rather than to start them, is enormous. I think it takes even more courage to abandon a project, to admit defeat and start anew. The miasma of unfinished manuscripts has created quagmires all across this writing nation.[7]

I ran across a colleague who is in residence at a research institute to finish a project in 2004, the very same project this person was working on a decade before—and with a fellowship for the *same* project at the *same* institution. So the academy is notorious for its role as both an enabler and a disabler. Can't finish that manuscript in the 1980s? Keep at it, into the 1990s. And when that doesn't work, just slog ahead—maybe into the next millennium! These are not isolated cases, as we can all tick off a half dozen scholars cosseted at major academic institutions whose lack of publishing productivity fits this description.

My complaint remains that those who want to talk about writing rather than actually write are often rewarded by the academy. Indeed, within the academy there is no compulsion to publish beyond ego—once that precious lifetime position is secured.[8] And research institutions fund scholars for uninterrupted stretches of time to work on their manuscripts, but provide no system of accountability. I am sure my grumbles are shaped by my own peculiar history and troubled relationship to the academy. And when I seriously contemplate these concerns, even I realize notions of "accountability" for a writer are absurd.

I am not suggesting that we be judged by the number of publications we rack up, or even our reviews or our sales figures.[9] But I am suggesting that there has to be an internal mechanism that allows us to balance all these demands while trying to keep intellectually curious and enthusiastic.

I admit that I succumb to obsession. I sometimes get an idea and won't let go of it—even if agents, friends, and publishers encourage me to move on. My stubborn streak has caused me minor heartaches and a few publishing blunders, but has created positive results as well.

When I have a passionate concern about some aspect of historical scholarship, it can take a long time for the payoff. I spent much of the 1980s working on Southern women—and one of the crucial factors I emphasized was that structures of racial and gender oppression were connected, if not interlocking. Thus, I would tease out ways of looking at these topics in tandem. I remember explaining to audiences the notion that Southern women had divided loyalties over the Civil War, which would often be challenged by an audience member. Then I would suggest that although many white Southern women supported the Confederacy, most African-American women in the South did *not*.

A pioneering band of scholars have made great headway on these critical issues—most heroically Nell Painter, who has always insisted that we recognize the multiplicity of Souths. She and others have made the *we* part for me in why *we* write. A consensus may not have been achieved, but again, a sea change is taking place, as complacent views that reflect only elite white male heterosexual perspectives are no longer acceptable as representative. We require different and better representations, those reflecting more diverse, more compelling, less soothing interpretations.

With all this diversity and compulsion, clearly the question of *why we write* has as many answers as there are writers. This writer knows she is addicted, she is driven, and when she ventures on uncharted terrain and loses her footing at times she needs to, as one of her subjects suggested, keep going. Increasingly it seems harder to recover from missteps, but she refuses to given in to cynicism. She has righteous indignation for those she feels poison the academy with their cynicism and contempt, but at the same time, some of her best friends are academics. She loves history and many historians, and is both exhausted and elated by continuing adventures into the past. As books come and go, she is not afraid that she will run out of stories, but fears she will run out of time.

3

WHY I WRITE

Timothy Patrick McCarthy

I love America more than any other country in the world, and, exactly for this reason, I insist on the right to criticize her perpetually. I think all theories are suspect, that the finest principles may have to be modified, or may even be pulverized by the demands of life, and that one must find, therefore, one's own moral center and move through the world hoping that this center will guide one alright. I consider that I have many responsibilities, but none greater than this: to last, as Hemingway says, and get my work done.

I want to be an honest man and a good writer.

—James Baldwin,
"Autobiographical Notes," in *Notes of a Native Son*

One of the many reasons to love James Baldwin, certainly one of the reasons *I* love him, is because he understood that writers are, essentially, paradoxical people.

On the one hand, writing is among the most private of enterprises. The writer finds a comfortable yet solitary space—"away from the world," as a friend of mine once put it—and fills it with artifacts of inspiration (or distraction): books, paintings, photographs, good lighting, comfortable furniture, even Internet access. Some writers, like me, also need music to guide them—the genius of Coltrane or Mozart, Ella Fitzgerald or Prince, even Tupac Shakur, serving as midwife to new forms of expression and aspiration. Or perhaps the writer prefers a sparser space, more silent, so that he or she can work alone, undisturbed. Every writer has a different way of finding and nurturing this space to help foster the kind of alchemy between inspiration and creation that is the essence of the writing process. But the space, the process, is nearly always a private one. This is true even when we write "in public," on the bus or plane, in the library or coffee shop, where we hardly even notice the people—or what's going on—around us. In other words, writing is a private enterprise precisely because writers, when writing, are *of* the world but not *in* it. In order to get our work done, as Baldwin urged us to do, we must commit ourselves to regular self-isolation. (If I were not so averse to clinical, or theoretical, categories for human behavior, I might even say that writers, when writing, are *antisocial.* We are, as one's grandmother might say, unfit for polite company.)

Yet writing is rarely, or even primarily, simply a private endeavor. Indeed, by definition, it is also a public one. Even the most stubborn purist would acknowledge that one writes in order to be read, regardless of whether or not this is the principal motivation for putting pen to paper in the first place. Granted, not all writing is *public.* Sometimes we write simply to record our thoughts, to chronicle our experiences, to work out complex emotions and reactions. Writing can help us make sense of things, and some writing, certainly, is better left unread. But there is a difference between, say, a diary and an essay. The former—except, perhaps, in the case of so-called "great" men who worry too much about how history will remember them—is not intended for public consideration. It is not meant to be read by others, and it certainly is not designed for publication. This is why a person can get so unhinged when a parent or lover, to say nothing of a complete stranger, looks through his or her journal; it is, fundamentally, a violation of privacy. Indeed, a diary signifies—embodies, preserves—the private by serving as a naked forum for one's unfiltered thoughts and experiences, one's intimate relations with others (I suspect this might be one reason why so many people don't keep one). On the other hand, novels, poems, plays, essays, speeches, and petitions—as well as other forms of what we might call public writing—function very differently. In various ways, they seek to tell new stories, to represent something in a different light, to make suggestions or demands, to illustrate emerging cultural sensibilities or political opinions, to intervene in things. Or, as Baldwin put it, "to examine attitudes, to go beneath the surface, to tap the source." In all of these ways, writing presumes and appeals to a readership, an audience, even a constituency; it establishes a *relationship* between the writer and someone or something else. At its most ambitious—and here I am thinking of something like the Declaration of Independence, or Harriet Beecher Stowe's *Uncle Tom's Cabin*, or the Port Huron Statement—it also seeks to effect some kind of social change. Thus, regardless of motivation, and far more often than not, writers seek to engage others, to use their writing to forge connections with the people around them.

Put another way, all writers want somehow to be *relevant*: to capture something new, to touch or inspire or provoke, to matter. And it is this desire for relevance—the need for some kind of meaningful connection with and impact on the world—that defines the writer's existence and determines his or her place in society. More to the point, it is the thing that both creates and sustains the tension—this writer's paradox—between private acts of creation and public influence.

* * *

One never knows how or when the past will become relevant. I suppose it's not at all surprising that I began to think harder about the influence of my own personal background at about the same time that I entered graduate school to study American history. I was an ambitious recent graduate of the Ivy League—the only, adopted son of working-class people; proof, to some, that the American Dream was still a reality— who now had the opportunity to get a couple more elite degrees. Notwithstanding the student loans I could and would defer, I was rich in another sense: I had done well at Harvard University; had studied with some of the most distinguished scholars in the country; had befriended some of the smartest kids of my generation; and was now, by virtue of all this, a member of the American elite. That said, given my conspicuous lack of power, money, and family connections, I hardly considered myself part of what the Marxists call "the ruling class." (I suppose, conveniently, that I was imagining "elites" to be better people, more benevolent, than "the ruling class.") Still, I was positioned well enough to have a very good life in America. Going to college, to Harvard, changed me. It was harder for me to relate to my friends and family from back home; sometimes, it almost seemed like we were speaking different languages. My outlook and options were different now, and so were my aspirations. I wanted more than I had growing up, and I wanted more than my parents and grandparents had, too. In many ways, I was more selfish, even greedy, and it showed. I even started to forget the lesson my parents taught me long before I had ever heard of Harvard: that it was far more important to be a good person than it was to be a successful person. That's what happens sometimes when blue-collar kids go to white-collar schools.

Graduate school orientation at Columbia University was a very strange affair. It was hot that day, very hot, the kind of day in New York City when you can see the steam rising off the concrete sidewalks. Still, Columbia's campus seemed somehow removed from it all, cooler and calmer than the city that surrounded it, so much so that walking through campus was almost like being *inside*. Fayerweather Hall, the history department building, is located in the northeast quadrant of the Morningside campus. ("Morningside Heights" is how Columbia admissions brochures refer to the neighborhood around it; it's a name, one longtime community activist later taught me, that really means *near, but not, Harlem*.) If you sit in the right classroom in Fayerweather, you can see out to Amsterdam Avenue, to Harlem. It's a breathtaking view, looking out over America's most famous black mecca from one of America's most prestigious universities. By virtue of reputation, at least, Columbia and Harlem seemed a perfect match: old, distinguished, important. It was too bad that the orientation program took place in a classroom on the *other* side of the building, away from Harlem; there was nothing to see there but graduate students reading thick books in a pristine little courtyard. (I remember wondering—I still wonder—if the choice of room wasn't intentional.) As the members of the entering class took their seats, with nervous energy pulsing through the room, we were greeted by several professors who seemed genuinely eager to welcome us to the program. "Ours is the nation's finest graduate program in history," one professor boasted, with no hint of humility in his refined British accent. "For nearly a century, America's finest historians have taught and been trained here," preened another. With this, they ran through the roster of Columbia luminaries—Charles and Mary Beard, William Archibald Dunning, Richard Hofstadter, Woodrow Wilson—and implied that we, too, might someday take our place in this pantheon. It all seemed so easy, within reach. This was a feast of inspiration for those who are moved by elitist sentimentalism, or who brought to the program an already heightened sense of their own destiny and self-importance. But for those, like me, with humbler roots and chronic feelings of intellectual inadequacy, it was an especially troubling ceremony. I was, admittedly, somewhat taken by all the lofty rhetoric, to say nothing of the institution's world renown, but I sat there wondering, deep down, if I really had what it took to succeed there. Of course, the same had been true at Harvard, where I somehow managed to elude all looming disasters (my tortured relationship with the Ivy League gives new life to the William Butler Yeats line, "Being Irish, he had an abiding sense of tragedy which sustained him through temporary periods of joy"). After a series of mundane logistical presentations about registration, advising, and the like, the orientation program was over. That is, except for the students who had received generous fellowship funding; they were instructed to pick up their stipend checks at some office on the other side of campus. Immediately, it became apparent who was who: "funded" students, many of whom had been feted and flattered by top faculty during the recruiting process, had satisfied smiles, as if they had won the lottery or something; on the other hand, "unfunded" students, many of whom didn't even know there had been a recruiting process, nervously gathered their belongings, trying hard not to look directly at anyone for fear their eyes would betray their institutional disadvantage. Desperately, the unfunded students tried not to draw attention to themselves; they wanted to blend in, to *pass* for funded. As it turns out, *that* would be impossible. These designations became an important part of our identity in graduate school: *Funded* meant you could get by all right; *unfunded* meant that you were screwed.

I left the orientation in a panic, sweating more from anxiety than heat. My advisor was on leave in England for the full year. I was one of the unfunded students (although I managed, successfully, to lie about it to most of my colleagues for quite some time). As a result, I had to take out even more student loans to pay for my tuition and books. I had saved just enough money from painting houses over the summer to cover food, rent, and cheap beer for the fall, but I knew that I needed to find a job soon to cover my expenses for the rest of the year. I entertained every possibility: bartending, cab driving, telemarketing, waiting tables. Honestly, I even considered some illicit and illegal options but quickly ruled them out because I knew that my Catholic guilt—already in full bloom from missing Mass too many times in college—would ultimately get the best of me. It probably goes without saying that I really resented having to spend my first day of graduate school—and far too many subsequent days, too—thinking about how to make enough money to avoid failing, slipping through the cracks. Sadly, my reasons for coming to graduate school—reading new books, taking new classes, touring the library, conducting original research, learning for its sake—were the furthest things from my mind.

As it turns out, that day, that moment of institutional differentiation between the haves and have-nots, was one of the most important days of my life. It is difficult to overstate how alienated and vulnerable I felt. For me, it was a deeply personal reminder of the combative, even destructive, nature of artificial—arbitrary, subjective—differences. It also taught me that elite people, far from being immune or opposed to such distinctions, are, in fact, usually the cause of them. (One might go so far to say that this is how the elites become members of the ruling class, and how they maintain their power once they get there.) Granted, I don't want to make too much of my own modest suffering and alienation—hell, I was still a doctoral candidate at Columbia!—but the point here is to emphasize that this episode finally made it clear to me why I had identified with people on the margins for so long: I was one of them. From my abandonment and adoption after birth to my unfunded status at Columbia, I had spent my entire life walking the thin line between rejection and acceptance. But I was lucky: I was an outsider who had managed to get inside. And this, I still believe, is why I am drawn so intensely to those who are made to feel different, those who have been left out, mistreated, or forgotten. I feel responsible to them, an old-fashioned sense of loyalty, solidarity. Or as we now say, *I got their back.* For most of my life, I had assumed that this was because I wanted to be *like* them; now I realized that I was *one of them* all along. I'd describe it as something akin to the difference between attraction (temporary, something you feel) and love (permanent, something you know); we often mistake the former for the latter, but rarely the other way around.

It was lunchtime, just after one o'clock, so I grabbed a slice of pizza and a Coke (what we graduate students liked to refer to as "the two-dollar meal") and walked across Morningside Park into Harlem. I knew exactly where I was going to: 117th Street and St. Nicholas Avenue, the block where my grandfather had lived as a child and young man. Grampa was first generation Irish American, born in 1909, and he lived on the same block in Harlem until he married my grandmother in the mid-1930s. There were a lot more Irish folk in Harlem back then—before "white flight" and the Great Migration changed the place—and many of them lived in this small neighborhood just east of St. Nicholas above 110th Street. By the time I got to Harlem, there were few traces of those days or those people. Nonetheless, the black folks who now lived in these buildings seemed to go about their lives pretty much the same way Grampa did back in the day: eating and drinking, loving and fighting, praying and singing, sleeping, and—of course—bitching about having to get up way too early to go to a job that paid way too little. They worried about the cops and about whether they could pay the bills and still take care of Momma and the kids, and they worried about how to stay warm in the winter and cool in the summer. In fact, Irish folks and black folks have always had a lot more in common than not, probably because they're both proud-as-hell people who spend a lot of time bragging about their dreams with the same confident intensity that often serves as a cover for the chronic insecurity and resentment that only hardworking, poor people can feel in their bones. This is why I could never understand why Grampa blamed Harlem "going to hell" on black people. I mean, after all, wasn't he one of the ones who left? After 1971, the year I was born, Grampa moved upstate to Albany. He never went back to the old neighborhood, said it wasn't the same anymore. That's why I decided to sit on his old stoop and have lunch that day: to get to know the place a little, to make a connection for myself—and for him, too. I suppose you could call it redemption, or reconciliation. Either way, my lunch on 117th Street helped to ease my anxiety; it also helped me to focus on where I came from rather than where I was going and if I was going make it.

Like so many children of recent immigrants, especially Irish ones, Grampa grew up dirt poor; in his old age, he used to joke about "not having a pot to piss in or a window to throw it out of." He dropped out of high school when he was sixteen, held a series of itinerant, low-wage jobs, and served in the army in World War II. (Unbeknownst to him, my grandmother was pregnant with my father at the time; by the time he came home, he was the father of an infant son.) In Grampa's company, I felt like an apprentice to a master—only instead of learning a craft, I was learning how to live life. I didn't mind the fact that he wasn't perfect. "There was only one perfect man, Timmy," he would say to me, "and they crucified Him." With this, perfection seemed to lose its appeal. Living like Jesus, that was one thing. But *dying* like Him? Hell no. Grampa was the best storyteller there ever was. He was funny, charming, and loud in all the quintessentially Irish ways, and he could excite a room simply by walking into it. Even on his deathbed, he loved New York City more than anywhere in the world. Thus, despite his regrets about what had happened to the Harlem of his youth, I think it would have given him a great deal of pleasure to know that his only grandchild was now living a stone's throw away from his old neighborhood—even if I *was* going to that "fancy college on the hill."

* * *

We're all shaped by the past. Indeed, history—the fact of *having* a past—is perhaps the one thing we all have in common. I would even go so far to say that because of this, we have a responsibility to the past, the same way that children and grandchildren have a responsibility, once they grow up, to care for the people who raised them. But we also have a responsibility to the present, to ourselves and our communities, to be active citizens in the world in which we live. This is especially the case, I think, in democratic societies where the rights of citizenship are guaranteed only because they have been won and earned by people who were willing to struggle and fight for them. There is, then, some truth to the familiar saying that if we do not learn history, we are condemned to repeat it. Or, as Baldwin put it, "I think that the past is all that makes the present coherent, and further, that the past will remain horrible for exactly as long as we refuse to assess it honestly." This search for coherence, this urgent need for honesty, requires that we engage history without feelings of nostalgia, or hostility, for "the way things were." Instead, we should seek to know the past so that we can better understand and appreciate how we arrived at the present situation, and so that we can, perhaps, move ahead without ignorance or invincibility—or worse yet, a false sense of innocence. Americans are famous, and also infamous, for their pretensions of innocence. We are a remarkably optimistic people (this is why Ronald Reagan, despite his vicious flaws, was so beloved), but we are also a people unwilling, or afraid, to fully accept our history. Indeed, it is a mistake to think that "youth" and "innocence" mean the same thing, for they do not. Despite our relative "newness," our history, like all histories, is filled with nasty imperfections and uncomfortable contradictions. These are the things we would rather forget, the blemishes we would prefer to cover up, and that is why Americans like to emphasize progress, the future, as if it were the only thing that matters. As long as we are better tomorrow, the logic goes, it doesn't matter that we were worse yesterday. But it does matter—or at least it should matter—and this is precisely why historians are so important. *But we need an optimistic history!* exhort the culture warriors like Lynne Cheney. Too bad there's no such thing. One cannot be optimistic about something that has already happened. (Indeed, the sooner we all admit we're not innocent, the sooner we become honest with ourselves and the better off we'll be.)

I suppose I was destined to be a very different kind of historian. Even as a child, I remember being unsatisfied with the way history was presented and taught, especially on days like the Fourth of July or Memorial Day, as if the point of American history, at least, was to make me proud of my country. I *was* proud of my country—I had no compelling reason not to be—but this felt like a very small reward for all the hard work I was doing in school.

I went to graduate school to study African-American history, to understand the central role that black people have played in shaping the United States. I was especially interested in the period of transition from slavery of freedom—the nineteenth-century struggles that led to emancipation—but I was also drawn, like so many young people in my generation, to the inspiring history of the civil rights movement, and to the explosive urban artistic revolution known as hip-hop. Thus, by the time I arrived at Columbia, it was clear to me that no one could possibly *know* America, past or present, without knowing black folks; it was the only way to comprehend this country's thick complexity, its tortured soul. Indeed, the answer to Ralph Ellison's famous query—What would America be like without blacks?—was a solemn, depressing one: America simply wouldn't *be* at all. To me, this was the fundamental point of the African-American writings I had read in college, and in a peculiar, subconscious kind of way, it was also the point of all those writings by white people—especially the "great" historians—who had worked so hard to diminish or ignore the presence, contribution, and influence of black people throughout American history.

As it turns out, I was not especially interested in documenting the atrocities of slavery and Jim Crow, although there was certainly enough there to keep more than one historian busy for an entire career. Instead, I felt compelled to address other matters: How have black people created a life for themselves—a culture, traditions—despite a long and painful history of white domination and oppression? How do we reconcile this long and painful history with the immense value we place on democracy? Why have African Americans, overwhelmingly, opted to stay in the United States, to fight for their full rights of democratic citizenship, and why did so many of those who did leave, like Baldwin, decide to come back? How did these historical experiences shape their understanding of the world, and how, in turn, have they shaped ours? How has the concept and reality of American citizenship—its radical promises of freedom and equal rights—changed as a result of the historic resilience, the patient and impatient struggles, of African Americans? Why do so many black folks *still* show a remarkable willingness and capacity to get along with white folks, even when so few white folks do the same? And finally, what happens to white people when they choose to ally themselves with black people in a common struggle to improve their society? In other words, what are the risks and consequences, and also the possibilities, of solidarity—friendship, love—between blacks and whites? These are the things that motivate my work.

Fortunately, I found the perfect job during my first year of graduate school, one that allowed me to investigate these questions—and other ones as well—in great depth. In January 1994, Dr. Manning Marable, the eminent public intellectual whom the late Ossie Davis once described as "our Du Bois," hired me as his research assistant at the Institute for Research in African-American Studies, an urban think tank he had founded at Columbia the previous fall. My fellowship covered tuition and fees, and it came with a monthly stipend, which temporarily assuaged my financial concerns. Aside from the money—which was crucial—this gave me the opportunity to go about my work in a setting that valued it. I once described the setting and its influence this way:

> It was during this time that everything began to change for me. My economic worries and personal woes soon gave way to genuine intellectual inspiration and political engagement. For most of those four years, I was the only white person in the office (my nickname was "Manning's White-Hand Man," a playful designation that once caused Lani Guinier to double over in uncontrollable, tear-filled laugher). This "minority" status was extremely important for me, and I suspect it was probably so for my colleagues as well. After all, this was the era of Rudy Guiliani and police brutality, welfare reforms and crime bills, the O. J. trial and the Million Man March. Race relations were not, shall we say, at their best. I was therefore fortunate beyond measure to live and work among Black people who genuinely liked and respected me at the same time that they challenged me to see the world through their eyes. Under Manning's learned and passionate guidance, the Institute was a place where we treated each other like family.[1]

In retrospect, I think my time at the Institute was the single most important influence on my career as a historian. Its emphasis on "living history"—on exploring the resonance, and forging connections, between the past and the present—provided me with the two most important lessons I learned in graduate school: first, that history was essential for fully understanding contemporary social experience; and second, that history could also be an important tool for social change. The latter was a bit more controversial, which is precisely what drew me to it.

All of this produced a profound tension in my life. In most of my history classes, I was being taught something else: to get "lost" in history, to develop a certain kind of "objectivity" with respect to the past that effectively divorced it (and me) from the world in which I was living. And I was being pushed—often against my will—to "focus" on my schoolwork, to not "get distracted" by other things (like labor strikes, police shootings, homelessness, war, and the like). Instead, I was encouraged to spend most of my time in the library, doing original research on nineteenth-century America, and then publish my work in scholarly journals circulating around the profession and, as it turns out, nowhere else. Many of my classmates and professors thought it was a waste of time for me to write a biweekly column on political affairs in the school newspaper; I can only guess what they thought of my volunteer work in Harlem, my labor activism, my basketball league, my trips to the South to rebuild burned black churches, my continuing involvement in the Big Brother program, and my teaching—a new thing for me that brought immense joy and inspiration during the worst days of graduate school. The problem was, life was going on all around me, in New York City and way outside of it, and I simply refused to separate myself from it. I couldn't reconcile spending hours at a time reading abolitionist newspapers and pamphlets, studying how antislavery activists fought to change their world, only to remain disengaged from my own. Late at night, as I returned to my office from the library, I would have to pass the images of Frederick Douglass, Fannie Lou Hamer, Dr. Martin Luther King, Jr., Malcolm X, and Sojourner Truth that adorned the Institute's walls. Sometimes I would rush by them, trying not to make eye contact, pretending that they weren't even there. But more often than not, I would stop and stare at them, taking in the various expressions—of toughness, anguish, pride, loneliness—that were contained in their faces. Whether I liked it or not, these images would stay in my head as I wrote late into the night. Periodically, whenever I took a break from writing to smoke a cigarette, I would sit at my office window, looking out over Harlem, blowing smoke into the solemn night air, and wondering what Malcolm or Martin—or the abolitionists—would think about what America had become. It was during these private times, all alone, that I also wondered, perhaps too selfishly, what they would think of me.

Thus it was during the dead of night—amid the private, lonely solitude of graduate school—that I had my revelation: I would write to be relevant. I would not divorce myself from the responsibilities of life any more than I would relinquish my rights as an American citizen. I would not be pulverized by the demands of life, or even those of graduate school. I would study history carefully so that I could both understand my country and teach my compatriots. And I would accept the risks that come from moving through the world with my own moral compass as my only guide. I would listen to people call me *un-American, treasonous, nigger lover, racist, crazy, faggot, communist,* and the like, and then I would show them why I am none of these things. I would pick my battles wisely and fight them to the best of my ability. I would love my enemies and cherish the few real friends I have. I would treat others as I treat myself. I would stop worrying about money and success, and I would remind myself of how much harder my grandparents had it back in the day. I would honor my parents and be grateful that they took me in. I would replace insecurity with courage so that I could stand alone when no one else was singing my song. I would speak truth to power, and I would use history to do so. I would write to change the world, one that I would be happy, at last, to live in.

If I managed to do all these things, I would be something that is rare in this world: a good person and an honest American. And that would be enough.

4

WHY I WRITE

Jennifer Morgan

I write because of my fundamental faith in the transformative power of narrative; not in the notion that simply by telling stories one might come to transformative truths, but rather that in unearthing the silences of the past we are necessarily involved in understanding the forces by which those silences were created and are maintained. I believe that writing history transforms the landscape of the present as much as it engages with the past. The women who are the primary subjects of my work have left few traces of their lives. The archives rarely house the words or even the experiences of women subjected to enslavement at the hands of colonial American slaveholders. And yet the archives themselves—conceived as testimony to the nation and built through the labors of the enslaved and the dispossessed—are dependent upon these women, and the men with whom they shared their lives. I am thinking here of the physical presence of the building. Who, for example, hauled those blocks of marble up the scaffolding? Who polished the floor on hands and knees? But, I am also thinking of the symbolic weight of authority the building continues to mobilize long after their lives have faded out of the collective memory that the archives allegedly maintain. In order to construct narratives organized around the lives of those who were not permitted to leave archival tracings then, we must reconfigure our archives. For me, the struggle to do so is the source of much broader political and critical transformations—both individually, and collectively. The writing that I do is intimately tied up in my desire to teach and in my conviction that through teaching and writing I am actively engaged in a transformative process.

I write because I can imagine no other tool through which I might address the reverberant violence of the past on my life and on the lives of those about whom I care. I explored other options, but they were neither as successful nor, importantly, as emotionally sustaining to me as writing. Through writing the histories of enslaved women in the Americas, I believe I have the potential to affect both the past and the present. The rhetoric of the past, the way that history is mobilized in contemporary political, social, and cultural life is ubiquitous. The women I write about have, fundamentally, been left out of that history. Insisting on their presence means, for me, insisting on the presence of contemporary actors who are "left out" of the stories we tell ourselves. Offering a revised narrative of the American past brings into sharp focus the ways in which history is part of the apparatus through which power has been and continues to be consolidated. But that is not all that is happening. When I write, I write not only about meta-issues, I write about real women.

Having come of age as a historian in the era of the linguistic turn, I can't succumb to notions of singular, recoverable, experiential, truths. I know that I must interrogate ideas of reality, embodiment, and materiality. And yet, there are real women whose lives I have accessed—however incompletely, however rooted more fully in the present than in the past—through my writing. Women like Clarinda and Kate and Parthenia and Arabell;[1] women who are positioned in our historical narrative as a result of my efforts to do so. I write because I believe that if I can simply breathe life back into the fragments that remain of their existence I will right a wrong. My writing transforms the archive. It stands as evidence both that the archive that denies Clarinda's existence is wrong, but also that another archival location is possible. I see my work as part of an ongoing conversation among historians, and I am saying, "Look at what is possible." As a colonial historian I harbor no illusion that I will ever find "new" evidence. The work I do is that of rereading sources—I tred on well-worn ground. But once I have asked the new questions—the questions to which Clarinda, Kate, Parthenia, and Arabell are at least a partial answer—I presume that others will too. My own work becomes part of a new casting of the archive and, to me, that is significant and meaningful. But there is something else.

When I was a junior at Oberlin College, Professor Adrienne Lash Jones told me that, actually, I couldn't write so well after all. Having been one of those minimally driven "A" students for much of my educational life, I was stunned to have someone take my work seriously, and to see through the meager effort that I brought to it. Moreover, here was a woman who I admired tremendously—the first tenured African-American woman professor in the history of the college, a gifted teacher, and a woman of incredible poise—and whose respect I actively courted as a student in her *Black Woman in America* class. In the bereft landscape of Oberlin, Ohio, here was a woman who I thought might tell me something about being a politically engaged African-American woman—about being an adult. My shame at being "called out" was matched, in retrospect, only by my gratitude. In essence, she brought writing to my attention. By forcing me to see that it was a craft, not simply a means to an end, she made it visible to me—initially as a source of shame, but ultimately as something much more powerful and central to the ways in which I see myself and my contribution in my chosen field.

Those were heady times—out in the Ohio wilderness in the early 1980s. My sense of self was undergoing fairly radical transformation as I struggled with my perplexing inheritance of mixed-race, middle-class, nerdy, Upper West Side New York City alienation. The act of reading was changing for me. From the age of six it had been a source of insulation: I was the chubby girl in the corner, wearing glasses, nose in a book, traveling across the prairie or worrying about Proginoskes's ability to help Charles Wallace. It was only at Oberlin that reading became a source of activism. I remember less about the courses I took than I do about the books I read: Paula Giddings's *When and Where I Enter*, bell hooks's *Ain't I a Woman?*, Audre Lorde's *Sister Outsider*, Cherríe Moraga and Gloria Anzaldúa's *This Bridge Called My Back*, Barbara Smith's *Home Girls*, Alice Walker's *In Search of My Mother's Garden*, Deborah Gray White's *Ar'n't I a Woman?* These texts continue to sit on my bookshelf, tattered and worn remnants of years of passionate and breathless reading. I wept over those books—tears of rage, of inspiration, of frustration, of love. Reading was no longer my escape from the world, but the way in which I could understand it.

After graduation, I moved to Boston (the Jamaica Plains neighborhood, of course) to begin work as a community organizer. Working with poor women in Roxbury around issues of fair housing and neighborhood safety I found myself challenged in a way that I continue to find difficult to articulate. I knew that what I was doing was important, crucial work, but I constantly felt impotent in the face of the avalanche of Reaganomic realities that these women tried to face down every day. In the absence of a college community of "baby activists"—doing work around divestment and antiracism—I felt that my reserves were utterly and completely tapped. The gap that separated me from these women was, in retrospect, outrageously obvious; but at the time it was an illusive source of struggle and pain that felt increasingly like failure. What I needed, and what those books I'd read in college laid a groundwork for, was a nuanced and careful critique of identity. I was yearning for poststructuralism; for subtle identity politics; for someone to name and define the in-between-ness, to theorize on the boundaries of identity, to help me to understand something of the alchemy of my loosely configured politics—of the intersections between my body and my subject position. And I was also yearning for pleasure. There was, in retrospect, very little in the way of joy in my life. And probably no one was too surprised to hear I'd decided to go back to school after two years in Boston. As I thought through the decision to pursue a degree in history I thought about teaching and about learning. I was increasingly aware of the gaps in my own education, and thought that, wherever it might lead me, a few years studying African-American history could only make me a better whatever it was that I was going to be. Moreover, teaching was something that made sense to me as an organizer. I couldn't very well imagine my future in some kind of an ivory tower, so obtaining a doctorate would be about preparing me to intervene as an educator.

Becoming a historian meant becoming a writer, although I didn't really understand that at the time. When I decided to pursue a Ph.D. in history, I did so with a vague sense that I might find both pleasure and transformative power through a reconfiguration of the past. I knew something (thanks to Adrienne Jones!) about the ways in which the histories of African-American women had been only most narrowly told. I knew something about the frustration and devastations of poverty and racism in the present. I also knew something of my own struggles to "place" myself as an African-American woman—but knew little about how to complete the process. Going to Duke University in Durham, North Carolina would do the trick, for there I could study history and enact a fictive return "home" to the place where my mother was born and my grandmother was raised. And that meant that I could learn something more intimate—something about the immediacy of my own past. I would study the club women, the lifting-as-they-climbed women, whose status and educational background was closest to that of my own mother and grandmother. But there could be no clear-cut story of proud and noble women in my past. A descendent of Spauldings and Burghardts—elite black families—on the one hand, and rural white Kentucky tobacco farmers on the other, I needed to explain the in-between-ness of my family's life, and therefore of my own, as it straddled the histories of race and class in America. My desire to claim a uniform African-American past could not be sustained, though it was a desire with which I remained in struggle for many years. Again, though I don't know how explicitly I understood this at the time, I think that in addition to what I knew about teaching to transgress, I thought that by getting a handle on that particular aspect of the past I might also better situate myself in my own present.

Sabbatical leaves being what they are, I found myself biding time my first semester taking courses in early American history and comparative slavery while waiting for the opportunity to study twentieth-century African-American history as I had planned. Early American history spoke to me in a way that in retrospect seems quite logical. The social and economic landscape of the seventeenth- and eighteenth-century Americas spoke powerfully to my convictions about the complexities of the past. But something else happened in those classrooms and, more important, in the archives. I had never imagined myself as a writer, in part, because on some level I knew that I didn't have access to the foundation level of introspection and self-scrutiny that the powerful novelists and essayists who'd sustained me in Ohio and Massachusetts did. And in that first rush of coursework, it was the reading, once again, that defined me. Now the essayists and novelists were accompanied by Hazel Carby's *Reconstructing Womanhood*, Winthrop Jordan's *White Over Black*, Edmond Morgan's *American Slavery, American Freedom*, Gary Nash's *Urban Crucible*, Colin Palmer's *Slaves of the White Gods*, Hortense Spillars's "Mama's Baby, Papa's Maybe," Sterling Stuckey's *Slave Culture*, Peter Wood's *Black Majority*, and Jean Fagan Yellin's edition of *Incidents in the Life of a Slave Girl*. It began to dawn on me that intense writing could come from the soul, but that the soul didn't need to be the object of inquiry. And with that realization came an understanding that I could access what I needed in order to write.

In the archives, I found what I needed in order to write—evidence. I used the North Carolina State Archives at Raleigh to write my first essay based on primary research, focusing on the lives of enslaved women in Edenton, North Carolina. I had no idea what I might find, and in truth, sitting there in the reading room I wondered if that enforced solitude might drive me mad before it yielded anything like a story. And yet, there among the genealogists and civil war buffs, I found with considerable pleasure what the person at the reference desk thought wouldn't be there. As I moved through the Ph.D. program, researching women's lives in West Africa, in colonial South Carolina and Barbados, in the British Public Record Office, the Barbados Archive, the South Carolina Department of Archives and History, the South Carolina Historical Association—I grew to love the process by which the sickening anxiety that *maybe that reference guy was right* was transformed into a triumphant sense that I had what I needed. I rarely had "eureka" moments, just a slow and steady accumulation of small pieces that together added up to something of momentous importance. I found evidence of women's lives. I found runaways. I found mothers and babies. I found enslaved people traveling eighty miles by foot not to disappear into the Great Dismal Swamp but rather to petition the woman who owned them to fire their overseer. In other words, I found complicated and muddled pieces of evidence that became the foundation for my own efforts to recapture the complicated and muddled lived experiences of the past. No heroes for me—I'd never been in search of heroes.

And later on, faced with bundles of notecards back in my apartment in Durham, I found that the process of putting their lives down on paper was among the most challenging and satisfying things I had ever done. For, remember, writing did *not* come easily for me. Back in the days before I knew the joy that is spell-check, I couldn't write a word without William Strunk and E. B. White's *Elements of Style*, a thesaurus, and a dictionary by my side. But this is where the pleasure kicked in. With the challenge of working really hard to perfect something that was actually quite difficult for me, I discovered something marvelous. Not only could I write, but with the right foundation—time spent in the archives asking questions that allegedly were unanswerable, and my color-coded five-by-seven note cards stacked to the right of the narrow-ruled yellow pad—I could actually do this thing well. And as I grew increasingly confident in my ability to write clear and well-organized paragraphs, I began to bring my sense of the complexities of racial categories and racialized violence to bear on the lives of these women who were, ultimately, so very far away from me. In the context of the poststructural, of the end of the singular and the denial of universals that marked my own entry point into the academy, I needed to do something different that tear down old heroes and erect new ones. I needed to presume that the complicated terrain I navigated in the present evolved out of an equal complicated landscape of the past. And so I wrote, and continue to write—with care and attention to the intricacies that shaped the past and the present and with an abiding faith that in doing so I am both mapping the past and reconfiguring the future.

Section II

The Process of Writing

5

DISORIENTED IN THE ORIENT:
A U.S. HISTORIAN GOES TRANSNATIONAL

Jung H. Pak

I left New York City in the fall of 2003 and headed for Seoul, Korea, where I was to spend the next ten months working on my dissertation on the Underwoods, a prominent American missionary family who has been in Korea since 1885. I thought I was fairly well prepared. From my vague recollections as a first grader in Seoul, some interaction with Korean-Americans in New York, and my research, I knew that Korea was a very conservative society and one of the most fundamentalist Protestant nations in the "non-Western" world. I packed what I half jokingly called my "Presbyterian" clothes—button-down shirts, slacks, loose-fitting sweaters, and absolutely no Britney Spears low-rise jeans or J-Lo midriff-baring tops. Two hundred pounds of research files accompanied me on the trip, along with a semifictional novel by and about a Korean-American woman who discovers her Korean "roots" through her investigation of her grandmother's life (even though I despise this type of ethnocentric, identity-obsessed literature). *How difficult could this be?* I thought. After all, most of my extended family was there, I could speak some Korean, and I was going as a Fulbright Scholar under the protective umbrella of the U.S. Department of State. Moreover, I knew which libraries to hit and which institutions to cajole for documents, and had a small list of contacts through my Columbia University advisor and friends. I was also armed with my fancy Columbia credentials and names of my famous dissertation advisors to flash around in case of emergencies. To top it all off, the executive director of the U.S.–Korea Fulbright program was an Underwood, a direct descendant of the first American Protestant missionary in Korea, and the reverence paid them by Koreans could only be compared to that toward the Kennedys in the United States. My mission: to show, as I wrote in my Fulbright grant application, that U.S. history "must be understood in its international context, cast off the idea that the American experience exists in a vacuum, and acknowledge the permeability of geographical boundaries." I was a subscriber to the concept of transnational history: that traditional, nation-based histories do not satisfactorily explain how global processes such as capitalism, religion, democracy, slavery, and the like have arisen from the constant intermingling of cultures, ideas, and peoples. I left for Korea to produce transnational history—to describe the movement of people (missionaries), their religion (Protestantism), their ideas (liberty, independence, moral rectitude, industry), and their impact on U.S.–Korea relations—but soon realized that I was part of the transnational project.

Transnationalism, as historian David Thelan described it, is the exploration of "how people and ideas and institutions and culture [move] above, below, through, and around, as well as within, the nation-state" and the investigation of "how well national borders [contain] or [explain] how people experienced history."[1] The field of transnational history, though it had been practiced most noticeably by scholars of immigration in the 1960s and 1970s, gained momentum in the late 1990s, inspired in part by globalization. By the time I left New York, a movement for the creation of a transnational history track in the Columbia history department was well underway, and departments at other universities had been active for several years.

My dissertation on nineteenth-century American Protestant missionaries in Korea who in the World War II era would become propagators of American political objectives in the early years of the Cold War in East Asia was an example of the transnational project. I sought to explain how religion—especially the evangelical Protestantism of missionaries like the Underwoods and their understanding of "America"— informed and transformed U.S. policy and how Cold War geopolitics undermined and/or confirmed missionaries' religious beliefs. My dissertation germinated from the knowledge that children of missionaries composed a significant percentage—disproportionate to the actual numbers of the missionary population—of the U.S. policy-making establishment. Intellectual historian (and missionary kid) William Hutchison and missiologists R. Pierce Beaver and Dana Robert, have posited that approximately 50 percent were involved in policy-making apparatus as area studies scholars, ambassadors, and U.S. State Department officials. In Korea, the only hot spot in the Cold War, missionaries and their legatees (including the Underwoods) became political advisors, and intelligence and propaganda specialists for the U.S. Military Government after the collapse of Japan and during the half decade before the outbreak of the Korean War in 1950. Two of the grandsons of the first Underwood in Korea (who arrived on Easter Sunday in 1885) were senior interpreters at the Panmunjom armistice talks from 1951 to 1953. On the non-governmental level, missionaries in Korea were important actors in organizing and implementing relief efforts for a population devastated by oppressive Japanese colonialism and wars, rebuilding their missionary institutions to ameliorate public health crises, illiteracy, and poverty.

A transnational perspective is pertinent to the understanding of missions and American foreign policy. As Robert has written, "the study of Protestant foreign missions leaned toward becoming a subsidiary of a political agenda, either in the service of national identity or in the debunking of the same."[2] Missionaries were either heroes of the American "errand to the world" in the 1950s or "cultural imperialists" laying the groundwork for American capitalist penetration in the 1960s and 1970s. Without disregarding the nation-state as a critical concept in foreign relations, or the American-ness of the missionaries, my dissertation sought to navigate through diplomatic history but also examine religion as a crucial component in its own right. The presence of missionaries inextricably tied U.S. policy in Korea with religion, and prompted Kim Il-Sung, then leader of the Democratic People's Republic of Korea (DPRK) and his son and successor, Kim Jong-Il, to condemn missionaries, in particular the Underwoods, for "trad[ing] in their crucifixes for rifles" and mowing down helpless women and children in the north.[3] The de-privatization of religion in the Korean context suggests that evangelical Protestantism was not simply a transcendent "truth," but a force that could strengthen or incapacitate the state. While U.S. policy makers saw Protestantism and its institutions as a strategic advantage in the war for hearts and minds, the DPRK and the Kims understood Protestantism as a force that could subvert their state.

My project necessitated creative use of documents and takes religion seriously as a transnational phenomenon. It involved examination of Korean converts, not merely dismissing them as "running dogs" of American imperialism or self-interested capitalists who sought to benefit from alliance with missionaries and the American agenda. Materialist motives do not sufficiently explain the entrenchment of Protestantism in South Korea (which holds the distinction as being the most Protestant nation outside the Western Hemisphere) or North Korea's persistent denunciation of missionaries and Christianity and its persecution of religious adherents. I sought to look at Korean YMCA/ YWCA records in Seoul, Korean-language documents deposited by missionaries and Korean politicians (many of whom were educated in mission schools) that reveal the nuances of political writings that were inspired by evangelical zeal to reunite the Korean Peninsula. The research also meant treating the Bible as a primary source since it informed the way the missionaries–cum–U.S. government agents perceived foreign relations and profoundly affected their behavior. I left for Korea imbued with the belief that I would be able to conduct research in the manner in which I had been trained at Columbia: comb through the stacks, mine the documents at repositories, collaborate with other scholars, and interview octogenarian missionaries who had been U.S. government agents in the mid-twentieth century. I was determined to "go transnational."

But what does it mean to go transnational? Like the missionaries and the intrepid travel writers of the late-nineteenth-century imperialist era, I felt like a pioneer; I was an American going abroad to illuminate an aspect of U.S. history. The missionaries' "calling" was to present the Gospel to a benighted land; my calling was history and the academic enterprise. While the steamship and imperialist jockeying for position in East Asia seemed to provide the means to go transnational for missionaries and represented tangible evidence of God's will, the Fulbright grant was my passport through the "open door." The missionaries of the nineteenth century were in pursuit of the Kingdom of God, and their sanction was delineated in the Bible; my covenant was with the Fulbright program. As a recipient of the grant, my referees and the national and international Fulbright committee that endowed me with the privilege believed that I would make an excellent "impression . . . abroad as a citizen representing the United States." Nationalism aside, I was determined to comb through the stacks, mine the documents at repositories, and so on in pursuit of "that noble dream" of historical truth and objectivity.[4]

There is a sort of idealism embedded in the pursuit of writing transnational history. The world is an open book—much like the way the missionaries described the "opening" of the Hermit Nation, as Korea was called in the nineteenth century, by the modern West and modernizing Japan. And by identifying the documents and their custodians, cultivating relationships with other scholars in the field, and through hard work, one could obtain as much information as long as the research money kept flowing in. The collapse of the Soviet Union and the opening of the previously closed archives touted by boosters and critics of globalization held the promise to pave the way for the idealistic transnationalist historian. I believed, as Thomas Bender wrote in *Rethinking American History in a Global Age*, that we need to get away from the artificial time and space boundaries of the nation.[5] I believed that historians of U.S. foreign relations, as I considered myself to be, had to investigate not only what one diplomat said to one another, but, as I wrote in my Fulbright application, that "whether an American is conducting Bible class in rural Korea or giving a Rochester lamp to a Korean friend, such acts have unintended political consequences and implications." In short, "the personal—and the interpersonal—is political" and international. U.S.–Korea relations and Cold War politics in general could benefit from the practice of transnational history because it acknowledges individuals like American missionaries "who were motivated above all by ideas, religion, and social or moral codes than on advancing any geopolitical or economic goals for their nation." However, my experience in Korea proved that the idea and act of transnational history were not culturally neutral. As a young woman and not a "pure" Korean by virtue of my American upbringing and imperfect language skills I soon found that "going transnational" was not as easy as Bender and others had proclaimed it to be. I became more and more "dis-Oriented" as I tried, in vain, to adhere to my concept of what it means to "go transnational." If geographic borders were not as important, then where was I "located"? If transnational history focused attention on the individual and the flow and exchange of ideas, it mattered who "I" was and what I represented.

The Fulbright program itself was a transnational project, designed by a U.S. senator who believed that cultural exchange would engender international cooperation and peace in the aftermath of the deadly conflict of World War II. "We must through international education," said J. William Fulbright, "use our talents and material wealth . . . not with the intention of gaining dominance for a nation or an ideology, but for the purpose of helping every society develop its own concept of public decency and individual fulfillment." The idea was to bring people from abroad to study in the United States so that they could go back to their home countries and preach the virtues of American life and civilization. Concomitantly, American students were to go abroad to study other languages and cultures—implicitly a part of the national security state. My application to go to Korea to research passed through the committee at Columbia, then to the National Screening Committee of the International Institute of Education (IIE), which administers the competition. The IIE then passed the application to the Bureau of Educational and Cultural Affairs of the U.S. Department of State and to the "supervising agency abroad" for review. Once it had the stamp of approval from the two agencies, the application landed on the desks of the J. William Fulbright Foreign Scholarship Board (FSB), whose members are appointed by the president of the United States. The path that my application packet took underscored the "national" aspect of transnationalism. The FSB maintains that "grantees are private citizens" and guarantees "the rights of personal, intellectual and artistic freedom as guaranteed by the Constitution of the United States."[6] But I was still expected "as a representative of the United States in Korea" to "demonstrate the qualities of excellence and leadership" and "fulfill the principal purpose of the Fulbright program: to increase mutual understanding between the peoples of the United States and the 140 [participating] countries."[7] For reasons related to my financial needs and career goals, I had to receive permission from the president of the United States and international agencies to fulfill my individual objective of completing my dissertation. It struck home what Charles Bright and Michael Geyer posited in their essay "Where in the World is America?"—that "we cannot escape the nation or dissolve it in to the ebb and flow of transnational processes."[8]

The nation-state is omnipresent, but transnationalism, as China scholar Prasenjit Duara has written, involves the study of "people's lived realities or ideological constructions that transgress, though they do not always subvert, the territorial boundaries of the nation-state."[9] The disorientation that I experienced early on in the Fulbright experience was as much the product of my doubts about whether I really was a representative of the United States as it was about the multiple lived realities of being Korean and American. I was the quintessential provincial New Yorker. Some may call my formative years in the Washington Heights neighborhood of upper Manhattan as a "postethnic" enclave where my best friend was Indian-American, my first bowl of borscht was laid before me when I was twelve, and matzoh and plantains were a part of my culinary vocabulary. My sister's best friends were African American and Filipino American. It was "beyond multiculturalism," as David Hollinger has described, in that I had parents who did not stress ethnic consciousness or Korean nationalism, and by implicitly imparting the idea that the world is open, gave my sister and me the freedom to choose our associations.[10] I went to school in a small liberal arts college in upstate New York that was a far cry from "representative" America where students of "color" comprised less than 5 percent of its undergraduate population. Similarly, Columbia University, an elite Ivy-League bastion, could hardly be considered "representative" of the United States, either. And the only time that someone accused me of being American was during my junior semester abroad in London in 1994, when a Briton heard my accent. Even in New York City, that symbol of cosmopolitanism, strangers and new acquaintances would ask me where I learned to speak English so well.

I was not American in Korea either. Nor was I Korean by virtue of my American upbringing. The simple act of flying across the Pacific Ocean complicated matters of time and space and demanded a reorientation to different realities. On the fifteen-hour flight, I passed through four time zones within the United States and then crossed the International Date Line, where I effectively "lost" a day: I boarded the plane in New York City on Monday morning and landed in Seoul's Inchon airport on Tuesday evening. Once I got an Internet connection—that quintessential emblem of globalization and the eraser of time, space, and geographical boundaries—I instructed my friends back home how they could reach me at a decent hour. My instructions were: "add two hours to New York time, change the A.M. to P.M., or vice versa" and after daylight savings time, which Korea doesn't follow, "add only one hour" instead of two. My instructions on calculating the time difference prompted at least one of my friends to balk: he quipped that it was temporally too complicated to keep in touch with me during my sojourn in Korea. To underscore the fact that time—and age—is relative, I was twenty-nine years old when I boarded the Korean Air flight at John F. Kennedy airport, but was thirty by the time I landed in Seoul because in Korea you're already a year old by the time you're born. I aged another year after the Lunar New Year in late January 2004. From September to January, I had "aged" two years.

When the first American missionaries arrived in Korea in the late nineteenth century, they thought, as Horace Grant Underwood did, that they had been "suddenly transplanted to the Middle Ages."[11] They had passed the newly created International Date Line, which was the product of an international conference in Washington, D.C., attended by scientists, railroad and telecommunications companies, and government officials in 1884, and arrived in preindustrialized Korea. It was clear from the Western calendar that the year was 1885 A.D., but it seemed as if Korea was more than "10,000 miles away" from the United States. One missionary stated, Korea was "2,000 years removed" from the twentieth century. He mused, "Why there was Rebecca coming from the well, there were the reapers, with Ruth gleaning among them, yonder the threshing floor of Boas . . . . That old patriarch over yonder leaning on his staff must be Abraham."[12] Another reported that in passing through Korean "scenes so ancient, so oriental, and so odd," that she "forgot for the time being the whir, rush, and nervous strain of modern American life" and felt as she had been "transported to the time and scenes during the life of Christ."[13] The Americans had been transported to the time of biblical antiquity.

Globalization had rendered the Korea of the nineteenth-century missionaries into a nostalgic illusion. I fully expected—naively I admit—the Korea of my childhood. Instead, I bought my coffee at Starbucks and met my Fulbright friends in front of McDonald's or KFC; Gucci and Louis Vuitton handbags were slung over the shoulders of every fashionable man and woman; incoherent English phrases adorned almost every T-shirt; and there was a chain store that sold knockoff Harvard and Yale University sweatshirts and varsity jackets. Almost all Koreans under the age of fifty had colored their hair. Instead of the sea of naturally black hair I expected to see in Korea, I saw a cornucopia of colors ranging from platinum blond to fire-engine red to the full spectrum of browns. The vast majority of Koreans of all ages had some sort of plastic surgery, from nose jobs to cheek and forehead reconstruction to calf implants. Plastic surgery is so endemic that women feel pressured to get their noses and eyes done to look more "Western" in the same way that women in the U.S get pressured to be thin and wear low-rise jeans. It has been the subject of documentaries and even Oprah herself did a segment on it. It was possible to see Korean women look like Jennifer Lopez and Britney Spears, whose posters adorned subway stations, bars, and music and clothing stores. In my conservative attire and jet black hair, I stuck out like a sore thumb.

Unlike the missionaries who had been embraced by the Korean monarchy beleaguered by the vagaries of East Asian imperialist wrangling at the turn of the twentieth century, my American culture clashed with the Korean perception of who really was American. The

Fulbright handbook given to us prior to our arrival informed (white) grantees that foreigners attract attention by virtue of their looks and "some enjoy being instant celebrities everywhere they go." Whenever I would go out to dinner or drinks with my white Fulbright colleagues, we often had drinks bought for us or would be toasted by a group of Korean men marveling at the way they spoke Korean. Korean-American grantees, on the other hand, may experience some mistreatment. Horace Horton Underwood II, the Executive Director of the Fulbright program in Korea, has written in the handbook,

> If a student was born in New Jersey, went to high school in California, speaks only English, and is a student at the University of Michigan, I, speaking as an American, know that that student is an American. But the average Korean will believe such a student is a Korean—but a "bad" one. If your parents were Korean, then you are too! If I can say "An-young-hash-im-niker" (hello), no matter how badly, Koreans will say how impressed they are by my Korean language skills. If one of those students makes even a slight error in grammar, particularly in the small suffixes that indicate politeness and relative place in society, they are criticized severely—because they are Korean, and Koreans don't make those mistakes.[14]

Koreans may have blond hair and green contact lenses to look more like Western actors, but their sense of the "essential" Korean underscores the "nationalism" part of transnationalism.

The concept of Korea as a "race" with its origins in the distant past of the mythical founder of the Korean nation, Tangun, is at the foundation of the belief in the immutability of the Korean identity or experience. The word *uri* or *woori* (our) is ubiquitous. I banked at Woori Bank and shopped at a convenience store called Woori Market. When speaking with Koreans, it was always "our" language, not Korean, and "our" country, not Korea or the Republic of Korea, and "our" company, not LG or Samsung. The dichotomy between insider and outsider coexisted easily with the Confucian concept of the five relationships: between ruler and the ruled, father and son, husband and wife, older brother and younger brother, friend and friend. The emphasis on the hierarchy of personal relationships had gender and age components. Korea, despite major legal developments in promoting equity between men and women, still remains a deeply patriarchical society. Although they may have graduated with top honors from a prestigious university, it was not uncommon to see women serve coffee to the men of their cohort who entered the company at the same time. They earn only 50 percent of the wages paid to men despite holding the same or similar positions. Women who dared smoke in public were rebuked or sometimes subject to physical assault by disapproving males, young and old. The rigidity of gender does not extend to non-Korean women, however. "Foreign-looking women," the Fulbright handbook stated, are accorded "honorary male status," and in a bar setting, are "toasted as one of the 'old boys' when everyone is deep in their cups [while] other women sit separately and are ignored."[15] Similarly, the Korean language is hierarchical—the use and misuse of the proper suffix that bestows honor and respect on the person spoken to could be grounds for silent censure or physical confrontation. The younger person cannot smoke or drink in front of an older person and status is immediately conferred according to age.

Two particular instances stand out that exemplified how the matrix of ethnicity, gender, and age played out in the transnational project. In October 2003, all American Fulbright researchers were invited to a fancy resort about two hours away from Seoul for a conference of the American Studies Association of Korea (ASAK). Of the sessions I attended, those presenting papers were American, Australian, Chinese, Japanese, and Korean. In the audience were members of the ASAK and representatives of the U.S. Department of State, which was one of the major sponsors of the organization and the conference. I found that those papers that dealt with American "culture" and political economy were extremely conservative and essentialist—especially the papers on American conservatism and family values. The paper on American conservatism argued that the United States has "succeeded" as an economic powerhouse because of its persistent "conservatives" who have advocated the free market and the individual work ethic. The paper implied that Korea has not been as economically successful as the United States because Koreans do not have this "conservative" tradition; Koreans, it argued, rely too much on the state. The family-values paper suggested that the transformation of the "traditional" nuclear American family into the egalitarian family arising from the 1970s rights revolts will lead to the imploding of the American family and, by extension, American culture, because women will no longer be concerned with child rearing. Generally, the commentators were insightful. The commentator for the family-values paper was extremely articulate and asked probing questions about the assumptions embedded in the paper. But the commentator on the American conservative tradition merely endorsed the arguments in the paper, despite its extremely contentious, ahistorical discussion. I was especially taken aback when one commentator accused his presenter of being a "pacifist" or an "environmentalist" without addressing the important biological and ecological problems posed by the paper. I thought the attack was unfair, so I raised my hand and in my clearest tour guide voice (for extra cash I lead historical walking tours in New York), I defended the paper. During the hiatus, that commentator approached me and said, in not so many words, "Where did a pretty young thing like you get such a loud voice?"

I would later become one of the paper presenters for the ASAK at a conference at a university in Seoul. To my glee, the commentator assigned to me was the scholar I had hoped for. My panel was composed of two other female presenters and two female commentators, making the discussant in my charge the only man at the six-person table. He offered important insight and suggestions, but to my chagrin he half-jokingly said that he felt "awkward" at being the only man on the panel. I was eager to talk to him during the break immediately following the panel presentation, but his focus was on another male professor and when he saw that I was hovering nearby, he merely said to his colleague, "She's a smart one." I never heard from him again despite repeated telephone and e-mail messages.

I did not write this essay to condemn or to point fingers. To be sure, I received some amazing treatment; my Columbia advisor's colleague gave me an office space and rendered invaluable advice, and my friend introduced me to a professor at another university who took me out to lunch, introduced me to countless other scholars, and e-mailed me on a regular basis to find out how I was faring. The Fulbright office, from the computer technology specialist to the receptionist to the executive director, supported me all the way. I write because I wanted to show by recounting my experience in Korea that the admonitions and encouragements of American scholars of the transnational phenomena did not apply levelly to all historians who undertake the transnational project. Historian Ian Tyrrell has warned that the dissolution of the Cold War geopolitical landscape has endowed the United States and American historians with a "new kind of empire," that asymmetry is inherent in the flow of people, capital, and ideas, and that power was skewed in favor of the United States.[16] On paper I had the power and the privilege: an Ivy League affiliation, the prestigious Fulbright grant, and the financial and institutional backing of the United States from Congress to the president. But power and privilege were diluted to some degree by the fact that I was a young woman and a "hyphenated

American," so perhaps Tyrrell's caution regarding the exercise of power and privilege applied more to some and less to others. It matters who you are; what nationality you represent; and your age, gender, and language skills. It matters how other cultures perceive the person attempting to analyze transnational forces.

Thomas Bender has enthusiastically written that historians "will be doing better history by being diligently empirical, accepting no artificial boundaries." But there are boundaries, geographic, national and cultural, and they are real. "The aim is verisimilitude, no more, no less," Bender proclaimed about transnational history, but my endeavors in transnational research suggest that truth seems to be more accessible to some, and less to others.[17]

6

NARRATIVES OF SEXUAL CONQUEST: A HISTORICAL PERSPECTIVE ON DATE RAPE

Jennifer Fronc

In May 2002, I began my dissertation research on sexuality and moral reform. As the librarian delivered the first large box from the extensive records of the Committee of Fourteen, New York City's most influential Progressive Era anti-vice organization, I was simultaneously filled with excitement and utter dread. What kinds of gems were tucked away in these boxes? And how on earth was I going to come up with fresh insights on social reform and morality?

As the days wore on, I began to worry. Frantically looking back through my notes, I panicked. I had nothing. I had copied a Brooklyn prostitute's terrible joke about why women wear black stockings (their legs were in mourning for all the stiffs that had been buried between them). I had put the stories about forced sexual intercourse in a separate file entitled "Rape?". I recorded the revelations of young shop girls—titillated by erotic poems, and frustrated because "good girls" weren't supposed to feel those things. But these didn't seem like the elements of a dissertation. And, in fact, a number of the stories never made it into the final version of my dissertation (except the prostitute's joke—I couldn't resist).

I was stuck. I had gone into the archives expecting to come out with a cohesive tale of early-twentieth-century prostitution reform organizations. I struggled with how to make sense of these sources, namely because they weren't what I had expected. I was so struck by the language—crass, passionate, violent—that I imagined belonged exclusively to us, the happy occupants of the early-twenty-first century, despite my training as a historian. I know that I prudishly gasped the first time I came across the word "fuck." I know I blushed and looked around when I read about the prostitute who, after fondling an undercover investigator's genitalia, exclaimed, "I bet you got jack!" Once I got past the prurient aspects of these materials, I realized that these sources did make sense if I took them on their own terms and if I recognized that the Committee of Fourteen's undercover investigators wrote them. These men and women were telling an important story—and through them, working-class men and women were telling *their* important stories. By recounting their interactions in particular subcultures (of exclusively male working-class saloons, largely female department store shop floors, and heterosocial dance halls and cabarets), the undercover investigators were unintentionally relaying a story about sexuality and sexual desire—one punctuated by bawdy jokes, dirty words, and references to sexual acts.

For instance, undercover investigator David Oppenheim filed a report on his visit to John Herbst's saloon. He initiated a conversation with a sailor, who told him about the last woman who had "picked him up." She took him to a hotel "all the way up" in the Bronx. He had to pay two dollars for their hotel room, and then she "had nerve to ask him $2 for herself." The sailor "belted her one in the nose instead and she stayed with him for the rest of the night without asking him for any money." He advised Oppenheim "to do the same."[1]

Oppenheim also investigated dance halls and cabarets at Coney Island. He made friends with an employee of Brooklyn Rapid Transit (B.R.T.), who told him that "you could find any number of girls laying around on the sand under the boardwalk."[2] The B.R.T. man said that "on a Saturday night you find a lot of young girls here dead drunk that men steered here, sc[rewed] them, then left them, he said there hardly a night him and other B.R.T. men don't come over here and get something."[3] About a week later, while investigating the Little Irish Association dance, Oppenheim observed that the conditions were generally bad. He concluded his report by remarking, "If an innocent girl should happen to come up here it wouldn't take these men long to get the best of her."[4]

So I had a collection of stories of forced sexual encounters as told by a male investigator and the other men he encountered in saloons and dance halls. But what did they mean? I hesitated to use modern feminist theories and explanations of rape and power, which tend to be totalizing and emerge out of their own political and historical moments. I found myself wondering what the female undercover investigators were discovering—from men or from women. Did they encounter similar stories? Was there a pattern?

I turned, then, to Natalie Sonnichsen, a female investigator for the Committee of Fourteen, who had been deployed to Macy's department store to test the "wages and sin" theory, which claimed that shop girls turned to casual prostitution to supplement their meager incomes. Sonnichsen's duty was to pose as a shop girl, befriend her co-workers, and get them to open up about boyfriends, sexual encounters and desires, and economic survival strategies.

Sonnichsen was quite adept at "passing" in this social milieu. She quickly became close with her female co-workers and got them to talk about local dance halls. She asked, in particular, about Frenze's, which had a reputation as a "tough" place frequented by a rough crowd. Sonnichsen's co-worker Anna said that she was not worried about getting a bad reputation by frequenting Frenze's or similar establishments, explaining that she believed that "if a girl is decent, nobody will touch her." Rose, on the other hand, said that she would not go to Frenze's "because it is enough for a fellow to know that a girl goes there, for him to draw his own conclusions as to her respectability."[5] Nowhere in this equation are there warnings of men taking sexual liberties, despite a girl's respectability or easiness.

Sonnichsen tested Rose further by telling her "an imaginary story of a friend of mine who had tripped up." Rose reacted with scorn, telling Sonnichsen that her friend was "a fool," and that girls should never "take any chances." When asked to elaborate on her point, Rose explained that she would make young men believe that she was "fast" in order to get what she wanted. She would have "a good time and at the psychological moment she would clear out." Sonnichsen asked her a number of questions, including if she had ever accepted silk stockings as presents. Rose answered, "no, because they'd want to put them on [me]." Rose then elucidated the early-twentieth-century social practice of "treating."

Historian Kathy Peiss has argued that women's low wages precluded them from participating in the emerging leisure culture.[6] Therefore, they began to trade sexual favors for "treats": food, clothing, and theater tickets. Peiss contends that this "widely accepted practice" allowed a woman to "accept [these goods] without compromising her reputation."[7] Peiss argues that sexual barter was a double bind: while it freed young women from old constraints, it also taught them that they occupied a lower socio-economic category, in which their bodies were commodities.

Elizabeth Alice Clement's recent dissertation follows up on Peiss's analysis of treating but claims that "treating opened up a new moral space between prostitution and chastity."[8] Clement argues that "women had *attractive* options about how to exchange sex for cash if they chose to do so."[9] Clement takes an optimistic view of this treating exchange, seeing this shift in working-class sexual mores as liberating for young women.

However, I see this as a pyrrhic victory. Women now had a place in commercial leisure culture, but it was at the behest of men. Treating (and prostitution, for that matter) was one of very few choices in a constrained labor market, determined and demarcated by gender, and during a time when women—working class and immigrant in particular—were occasionally forced by circumstances to sell their bodies. I see very little that is liberating about having to sell one's body in order to feed children, pay rent, or get a new pair of shoes.

Moreover, Rose also sheds light on the sexual double standard of this period: specifically, that young women themselves were responsible for policing these arbitrary moral boundaries, and men were expected to push those boundaries. If a man succeeded in violating those boundaries, then it was the girl's fault. Young women like Rose, who believed that they could "clear out" at the appropriate moment, demonstrate the tensions that women must have been experiencing—and suggests how vulnerable women were when dealing with men. These young women may have known their moral boundaries, but they may not have counted on men like the sailor, who punched the prostitute in the face, or the men who got women drunk and dumped them under the boardwalk. These were dangerous situations that may have resulted in forced sexual intercourse, no matter how moral and principled the young woman was.

Sonnichsen learned from Anna, Rose, and others how young, working-class women navigated the new leisure landscape and negotiated between sexual desire and social mores. But their confessions and justifications lead me to ask: did society, by not providing room for female sexual desire, create conditions for men to sexually take advantage of young women, like in Oppenheim's reports?

The problem here, for feminist historians, is to try to step beyond the "sex debates" of feminism, and try to come up with a historically grounded discussion of the problem(s) of sex in the first decades of the twentieth century. In these stories, young women found themselves in a position to negotiate with men but not on an equal footing. Men had money; women had their bodies. Women wanted the money (or things the money could buy), and men wanted access to women's bodies. However, these exchanges did not go off as seamlessly as other historians have suggested. In the case of Oppenheim's Coney Island report, drunk women in the company of drunk men may have found themselves engaged in sexual contact they did not want.

Interestingly, the women who speak through these reports were not talking to each other about unwanted sexual advances. They counseled each other not to drink too much, or not to attend particular establishments because they may be perceived as "fast," but they were not warning each other, or speaking from the experienced standpoint of victims of forced sexual encounters. Is this because it didn't happen? I doubt it. But I do suspect that the sexual double standard (which held that girls must guard their reputations and blamed them if they were compromised) created an atmosphere of shame and silence to accompany any unwanted sexual encounters. While the women in these records were silent on these matters, the men were not.

Through the records of the Committee of Fourteen's undercover investigators, I learned that the treating relationship and sexual barter were widespread, acknowledged, and discussed openly in early twentieth-century working-class New York. Young women as well as men spoke to one another about the treating relationship. Male undercover investigators used conquest stories of forced sexual activity to demonstrate camaraderie and masculinity, as well as to forge a relationship of trust between and among the men they were investigating. The investigators' stories about sexual coercion were not just invented on the spot; instead, they picked up and circulated stories told by patrons and bartenders. And, unfortunately, these investigators were keeping stories and strategies of sexual coercion in circulation, stories which may have had very real—and unintended—consequences for young women.

For example, on the afternoon of July 8, 1913, "L" entered the bar of the Avenel Hotel. Henry was bartending.[10] They greeted one another, and Henry asked L how his girlfriend was "feeling." L replied "that she looked and felt as good as ever." Henry responded, "'Still after her, eh! You must like her.'" L answered in the "affirmative, adding that she was a fine 'chicken,' that [he] had spent all kinds of money on her and would get her in a hotel do or die."[11]

Three weeks later, L returned to the Avenel and Henry was, once again, behind the bar. Henry "immediately engaged [L] in conversation...asking whether [he] had gotten that 'chicken' yet." L said not yet because he was "afraid to take a chance in the grass or a hallway as she might yell and have me pinched. The only thing to do is to get her in this back-room...force her upstairs and then she couldn't squeal." L concluded with a somewhat desperate request, appealing to Henry's manly instincts: "Can you fix it for me, Henry?"[12]

One month later, L was sent back to the Avenel and found the barroom empty, save for Henry.[13] The bartender remembered him and, as L documented, "wanted to know what happened with 'my girl.'" L explained to Henry "that she would not enter a hotel for fear of being observed by a friend or an acquaintance." Henry counseled L that "it's easy with cases of that kind.... All you have to do is take her upstairs by the 124 St. entrance and she won't be wise." Because L had spoken openly of his sexual frustrations and his designs on his hesitant girlfriend, Henry was then willing to offer advice on how to have sex with reluctant partners. He even "reminded [L that] he would lend every assistance" so that he may "accomplish [his] purpose."[14]

On July 8, L returned and told Henry that he planned to take his girlfriend to "Pabst's Harlem some night, get her under influence of liquor, take a taxi, and rush her into a hotel before she would realize it."[15] Henry confided in L about Lizzie, a "married woman...who was taken by him to St. George and walked to Inwood where he forcibly had sexual intercourse with her. Telephoned her three days later and took her to a hotel—after that it was easy." Henry also "reminded [L] how simple it was to 'get to' women who frequent saloons unescorted. In one case he took a salesgirl working in...125 St., from [the] back room [of a local saloon] to a hotel in the vicinity and had intercourse."[16]

The interactions between these two men suggest a frightening reality for working-class women: if they went out drinking with men, they were considered sexually available. Further, unescorted women were considered fair game for sexual coercion. For L, as the recorder of these stories, and Henry, as the teller, the distinction between rape and consensual sex barely exists. In these stories, the men were free of the taint of sexual immorality; the unescorted women, drinking in public, were portrayed as sexually available, whether or not they consented to sexual activity.

In the records of the Committee of Fourteen's department store investigation, where we best hear the voices of the working-class girls like Anna and Rose, we hear them talking about girls who are too painted, girls who have gone wrong. There is a code among them; they do have definitions of respectability. They emphasize steadies and engagements, and they talk about their steadies having other women—and those appear to be the women with whom their steadies have sex, not them. But they do not talk about rapes and seductions and force and violence. There does not seem to be a conversation about being careful, or being raped or assaulted. There seems to have been a code of respectability among the women (and a modicum of shame) that would prevent one from talking about being raped: if a woman was raped, it was her own fault because she had behaved too familiarly. There was not a discourse of rape among the women, only among the men.

What is my responsibility as a historian, as a feminist? Is it to my sources? Or to my political beliefs? These questions tormented me as I tried to write the conference paper upon which this piece is based. But what was really bothering me, what reverberated every time I sat down in front of my computer to write, were the voices of the young women who had been assaulted, who wanted to let their boyfriends kiss them, who just wanted things to be different.

Maybe the Committee of Fourteen's undercover investigators didn't do anything for these young women—maybe they could ignore the cries of "stop" and "don't." I can't. Maybe no one did anything for these women in the wake of these unwanted or coerced sexual encounters—indeed, there did not seem to be a vocabulary that would allow for any recourse—but maybe I can do something. Maybe I can tell you what happened to them, maybe I can make you hear them calling out "stop" and "don't." Maybe we can have a conversation about what happens to women in a culture that does not permit them to own and express their sexual desires safely, without fear of earning a "bad" reputation. Maybe we can talk about what happens in a culture where one's gender proscribes and prescribes certain privileges and positions of power. Maybe we can talk about a history of the discourse of sexual violence and the cultural cache that comes to those who can speak that language, and think about how that still reverberates to this day.

7

HER HEART, MY HANDS:
WRITING AN INTIMATE LIFE

Caitlin Love Crowell

The title of this essay owes itself to legal theorist Patricia Williams's discussion of her search for her great-great-grandmother's history. She had little information to go by—"slave, female" is the only title that history has left this woman. Williams relied, therefore, on writings by and about Austin Miller, the man who bought her great-great-grandmother at eleven and had her pregnant by the age of thirteen. "I am engaged in a long-term project of tracking his words," Williams writes, and "of finding the shape described by her absence in all this."[1] This notion has rattled around my conscience since reading it; it is a great summary of what historians do. Williams searches everywhere for—and finds—the ghost of her great-great-grandmother and the concrete past of her great-great-grandfather, "her shape and his hand." In politics, in law, in sex—everywhere is evidence of her invisibility and his power.[2]

In my research I seek the space left by another sort of absence: I am looking to find the shapes of black women's hearts. Much good scholarship has been wrung from the extraordinary work that African-American women activists did in the nineteenth and twentieth centuries, but on the whole it concerns itself with the public, professional careers

69

of these women. What of their interior lives, though? How did a black woman activist like the renowned Anna Julia Cooper experience love, loneliness, and sexuality? How did her professional life shape her personal choices? What did it take to move her? I contend that if we ever hope to understand a history so complex and illuminating as hers, or to draw on it in our own lives, we must attend to the soundings of her heart.

Imagining the intimate worlds of our subjects will almost always be beyond our abilities. Fumbling, we try to sketch out stories, and if they fall short of their mark we may never know. It is an enormous responsibility, assuming the right to delve into someone's private life and to write the story that that person cannot correct. Worse, however, is evading that responsibility, and leaving blank all the spaces that make up our subjects' emotional and romantic and sexual selves. To see the absence, and to leave it empty, seems the greater sin.

> It's hard to imagine how unremembered we all become,
> How quickly all that we've done
> Is unremembered and unforgiven.

> —Charles Wright, "The Woodpecker Pecks,
> But the Hole Does Not Appear"

Born a slave in Raleigh, North Carolina, in or around 1858, Anna Julia Haywood Cooper eventually made her way to Oberlin College and then into a teaching career. An activist, a writer, and above all an educator, she served as principal of M Street, Washington, D.C.'s prestigious African-American high school. Cooper became famous in her time for her race work. In 1892, she published *A Voice from the South*, a series of essays dealing with race and gender inequality in the United States. Eight years later, she addressed the Pan-African Conference in London. She helped establish Washington's YWCA, became an honorary member of the American Negro Academy, and associated with the leading black intellectuals of her time. In her sixties she earned her doctoral degree, and in her seventies she cofounded and ran Frelinghuysen, a pathbreaking community college for adults. Her writing, now revisited, is taught nationwide, and a small street in Washington, D.C. bears her name.[3]

So far, so good: this is what we know and document and discuss. But it is not her activism and professional life that concern me here, except insofar as they shaped her private life. Rather, I want to talk about trying to write the story of her intimate life. What intrigues me is a life not found in her papers, or in surviving legal documents.[4] My own public record, of documents and photos and letters, does not capture the entire life I lead, nor even the most important part. Why then do we pretend that the surviving documents about Anna Julia Cooper capture her real life, her whole life? Why do we not ask more about the workings of her secret heart?

Cooper's intimate life was a long history of love and loneliness, relentlessly intertwined. Both she and her mother were slaves in Raleigh; both were owned by Fabius Haywood. Neither talked publicly about Anna's father, who was probably Fabius himself. In 1877, she joyously married fellow teacher George Cooper and set about the task of living an emotionally and socially worthwhile life. Two years later, however, his death made her a twenty-one-year-old widow. Cooper carried on, teaching and establishing herself as a significant commentator on race matters. In an 1892 essay on women and higher learning, she addressed a popular question concerning female education. "Is the intellectual woman *desirable* in the matrimonial market?" she queried. "This I cannot answer. I confess my ignorance. I am no judge of such things."[5] Yet, who better to judge such things? By then she had clearer claim to the title *intellectual* than did most Americans, and she had been widowed for well over a decade. Bold enough to repeat the question, she wasn't brave enough to answer it.

Widowhood did not mean a life alone. Upon the death of a friend from Raleigh, Cooper assumed responsibility for two foster children, John and Lula Love. She brought the two with her first to Washington, and then to Hampton Institute in Virginia, and finally back to Washington, where she and John took jobs at M Street. Both brother and sister lived with her until she and John were accused of having a love affair. Amid parents' protests and mounting gossip, Cooper and Love were let go from their jobs and moved on to different homes in different states.

Getting at her feelings about these events presents enormous challenges. What did it mean to her to come to consciousness as chattel to her father, to imagine that her mother's lot might someday be her own? Was her apparently ideal union with George Cooper blessed by amiability and a satisfying sex life? When he died, did she wonder whether she would ever fall in love again? Or did she, with John Love? Some of these questions are unpleasant even to write, and I believe a good number of historians would question why they should be written at all. But they are not prurient, they are not just gossip, and they are not to be taken lightly. They lie close to the center of her identity, just as matters of intimacy, sexuality, and emotion lie near the core of our experiences in the world. Anna Julia Cooper may have stayed up late thinking about justice and culture and politics, but I'll bet that thoughts of sex and love and loneliness kept her up as well.

The study of personal lives necessarily addresses questions surrounding public and private spheres. Untangling the intimacies and friendships, the loves and heartbreaks and the loneliness of black women activists relies on understanding the social and political backdrops against which they took place.[6] By "intimacy" I do not mean to suggest that the matters I explore here—sexuality, romance, love, friendship—were somehow closer to the hearts of women activists than their public political aims. Cooper herself would not have accounted her love life more important than her work for justice, and often she appears to have sacrificed the former in pursuit of the latter. Nor do I propose that we can draw a line of demarcation; if recent feminist history has taught us anything, it is that we cannot labor under the illusion of truly separate spheres. But Anna Julia Cooper, like many of her sister activists, spelled out a means for envisioning politics dependent on, and theoretically cognizant of, the personal. It falls to us, then, to explore the dimensions of those politics, and to ferret out the intimate histories that guided her public choices.[7]

Just as important, we should recover the personal as the personal; private lives hold lessons of their own. In our efforts to establish the validity of intimate experience as a matter of public concern, we easily forget that we should not need to justify an interest in biography, in intimacy, in the sometimes mundane, sometimes extraordinary details of the lived life. We need to look at Cooper's private life not only in order to more fully understand her public self, but because the workings of her heart and her home themselves deserve a hearing. History ignores the realm of the personal at its peril, for without nuanced understandings and analyses of private lives and needs, scholars can offer only an impoverished and diminished conceptualization of their subjects' public worlds and works.

Cooper might not have agreed; indeed, like many she went to great lengths to ensure a separation between what she offered to the world and what she kept to, and for, herself. This poses a twofold dilemma: not only are resources scarce, but sometimes uncovering them seems to contradict directly the wishes of our subjects. Historian Darlene Clark Hine most beautifully articulates this idea in her essay on the "culture of dissemblance" that some black women fostered to protect their inner selves from the predations of a brutally sexist and racist world. Sexuality in particular and inner lives more generally, Hine suggests, were "those issues that Black women believed better left unknown, unwritten, unspoken except in whispered tones." Yet keeping those secrets leads to "misplaced emphases" in histories of black women; it threatens, ironically, to replicate the silencing if the cost of restoring women's voices is too dear.[8]

> Well, the world's open. And now through
> the windshield the sky begins to blush
> as you did when your mother told you
> what it took to be a woman in this life.

> —Rita Dove, "Exit"

Long before she burst with love for George Cooper, and perhaps for John Love, Anna Julia Haywood knew about the ugly intimacy of Fabius Haywood's household. Here was a place where illusions of family, love, and sexual morality came up against the truths of slave life: Anna Julia was born the daughter of Hannah Stanley and her owner, Fabius Haywood. Although neither mother nor daughter seems to have explicitly acknowledged her paternity (and of course circumstances make a mockery of the term *paternity*), Cooper's silence spoke nearly as loudly as her words might have.

This was, among other things, a colonial intimacy, sticky in the heat of Raleigh summers. Hannah Stanley may have given her daughter explicit details, or may have chosen veiled threats (watch out!); she may have let sadness or anger speak for itself. We won't know and ought to be particularly circumspect in spaces like these, where what we now think we know about psychology can tempt us to draw modern conclusions about the very different hearts and bodies of people in those times. What Stanley's daughter learned eludes us, but this was where she learned it, in a household that bought and sold families. Haywood and his family and acquaintances did a booming trade; bills of sale and affidavits outline the relentless coming and going of black bodies. Anna Julia may have known Lean and her four children, or Betsey, or John Buffaloe. Hartlep had cost $999, while "Henry—a slave for life" had commanded just $600.[9] Her mother could be made to reproduce for free, if she survived the process.

Emancipation could not have erased what Anna Julia knew about sex and race; she could not have forgotten the lessons written in Fabius

Haywood's hand. Her politics, defending the full humanity of women and of African Americans, insist that she knew what to learn from her own past. I would argue, though, that her intimate identity in general points to a heart that knew what to want, and how to want it in the face of a world largely opposed to black women's happiness.

Cooper had grown up loving beauty, and loving to be in love. Bookish and starch-collared, she nonetheless felt deeply, often physically, the effects of her emotions. There are clues to her excitement, such as those in her recollections of meeting with others she saw as intellectuals. Yearning for stimulating environments, Cooper hosted a Sunday evening salon: the famed composer Samuel Coleridge-Taylor came, as did Frederick Douglass's wife Helen, and her friends the Grimkés, minister Francis and writer Charlotte Forten.[10] Here, she admitted, the discussion roused her passions: at the thought of a good debate, she felt as a "war horse, quivering for the fray." Stimulating conversations, and the joy of being taken seriously, made Cooper feel like an "Atlantean swimmer, buffeting angry billows with affectionate strokes of leg and arm."[11]

Picking through her language, I try to separate the hackneyed from the heartfelt. One might dismiss this as just another series of clichés—anyone who has ever read mediocre writings about ancient wars knows about quivering for the fray. But I think Cooper meant what she said—I think that she thought about velvety nostrils and hot breath and hearts racing with terror and anticipation. Why else choose such purple phrases? This was book talk, and her evening promised, at most, the flush of pleasure at an argument well made. Yet she quivered like an overheated stallion; she dreamed of taming an ocean as water swept down the length of her thighs. These are not the words of someone who doesn't know her own body. And Cooper was a woman in love with words, a richly rewarding affair that would last all her life. She spoke and taught Latin and Greek, and wrote her dissertation in French at the Sorbonne. And of course she employed English that was as eloquent, gracious, cutting, or funny as she wanted it be. Not having to resort to language that conveyed less or other than she felt, she did not.

Consider her calling card: graceful script with her name, her at-home hours, and her . . . motto (if it can be called that): "*Je meurs où je m'attache*," the cards read, capped with a little stem of ivy.[12] Naturally the linguaphile chose French, the romantic language she so loved. It is a difficult phrase to translate graciously, anyway, meaning "I die where I stick." In the language of flowers, it is the phrase associated with ivy: it indicates eternal fidelity but has a parasitic dark side, as well. Ivy lives symbiotically. Eventually its curling vines will fell the sturdy trees that hold it up, but it will never leave, and it will die along with the tree, or perhaps outlive it. I suspect that Cooper meant to suggest steadfastness, faithfulness, and above all a heart that would be true to the death. *Comme le lierre* (like the ivy), a lover might proclaim, *je meurs où je m'attache*. But to whom, or what, did she attach herself?

It is hard to imagine and harder still to prove (let alone to write) what happened to Anna Julia Cooper's body. The closer one looks, the more elusive evidence about sexuality becomes. The things we believe we know—that people have a sex drive; that chemicals course through us, impelling us toward physical involvement; that humans long for intimacy—fall in the face of a sheer absence of conclusive evidence. In a vacuum, we imagine, we could test this. But we can never establish a control for our thought experiment; our characters will always exist amid roiling, competing, and inescapable social circumstances. More difficult still are the assumptions we make more quietly: that people's bodies remain fairly constant, and that as a result their behaviors remain knowable. No sooner do we hold these ideas up to a harsh light, though, than they begin to fall apart. We have little evidence of what sex was like for our subjects; we do not know what their bodies were like, or how they felt pleasure or pain. Even when we have what appears to be evidence (love letters, say, or writings describing a passion that seems recognizable), contingency pulls us up short. Sexual pleasure and emotional pain, insofar as we can recognize them, are socially constructed. The shape of our bodies has changed; so have our clothes, and the technologies of sex. So just as modern political ideas do not apply to older historical eras, current understandings of sex, passion, and love do not apply to our subject's intimate feelings. Too often, though, the result has been that historians do not apply any ideas at all.

Cooper came from a world of circumscribed sexuality and from a society, with its late Victorian, middle-class mores, that struggled above all to limit and contain desire. She was a woman of strong desires, though: the desire for racial equality that shaped her activist career; the desire for women's progress that led her to write *A Voice from the South*; and the desires for home, happiness, education, and company that were nothing if not profound. Yet as she wrote, Cooper also knew about surrendering to "love's lunacy," knew how it felt to "yearn for the sacrificial altar to prove by dying the undying attachment of conjugal devotion."[13] Anna Julia Haywood had met George Cooper at Saint Augustine's Seminary in North Carolina, a black preparatory institute, where he had moved from the British West Indies to study for the priesthood. By 1877 the nineteen-year-old schoolteacher had pledged her heart to her colleague.[14] Little remains to document the marriage, and one is left to imagine the wedded world of George and Anna. Two years later, though, she was a young widow who knew about conjugal devotion, but she no longer had a husband.

Let's look at Cooper's paean to her dead husband. Over fifty years after his death, she would donate to the school a beautiful stained glass window of St. Simon of Cyrene in George Cooper's honor. Anna also penned a poem, praising the ideals of Simon of Cyrene and his

> heart that ached to give
> All of its soughing pulses
> that brother man might live.

Here's the Cyrene—we can practically hear the soft thud of his heart beating. Every bit as manly as he is holy, he is pure, but look how

> His brawny arms knew burdens
> His big, broad shoulders, bent
> To many a loving service
> A willing lift had lent.[15]

Phew! All that brawn and bicep, and soughing pulses! The saint elevated her senses, but the man could lift her body like a feather. Was she really thinking of St. Simon here? Or George?

Not that Cooper had ever spoken of such matters. Instead, she suggested that woman might live by books alone. Singing the praises of intellectual development, she explained that thereby women's horizons broadened. No longer, she claimed, "is she compelled to look to sexual love as the one sensation capable of giving tone and relish, movement and vim to the life she leads." Instead, she might look to Homer, Virgil, and John Milton. Or "she can listen to the pulsing heart throbs of passionate Sappho's encaged soul, as she beats her bruised wings against her prison bars and struggles to flutter out into Heaven's æther, and the fires of her own soul cry back as she listens. 'Yes; Sappho, I know it all; I know it all.'"[16] Nineteenth-century prose or no, that's exciting reading. Enough to make one wonder, in fact, what a woman might mean as she cried out like that.

She might mean that she wanted to be back in a romantic relationship. Educated women might be ill fitted for the marriage market, she had acknowledged, but that didn't mean they were always content being single. By the turn of the century, when she was forty-two, her foster son John Love, nearly thirty, was on his way to becoming a scholar of race relations in his own right. When Cooper had moved from Washington to Hampton, Virginia, Love and his sister had moved with her. When she moved back to the capital, so did he. When she traveled to London to address the Pan-African Conference, he went, too. When she became principal of the M Street School, he taught there. And that's where gossip caught up with them, living together, working together, and, people suggested, *being* together.

The gossip mongers may have completely fabricated their charges. Cooper's relatively powerful position as a black female school principal drew enough censure to spur criticism. A very public figure, Cooper depended on unimpeachable moral credentials to allow her space as a race spokeswoman and youth educator. As a widow, she enjoyed a small bit of leeway, but definitely not enough to misbehave with a man, least of all a much younger man who worked and lived with her. Neither her widowhood nor her status as John Love's foster mother protected her from rumors. Amid swirling accusations of school mismanagement and moral turpitude, the two were let go from M Street, and they went their separate ways. She headed out to Lincoln University, in Missouri, where she taught languages, and he continued his race research and went to work for the National Association for the Advancement of Colored People.

What is served, however, by not questioning what happened here? We would do well to remember that history offers up an endless parade of characters who have refused to abide by the social strictures under which they lived. If Annie and Johnny (as they called one another) were in fact in love, did that love constitute resistance? Alternately, if they did not touch each other, we need to take account of the forces that might not have allowed them to act on that possibility. Historically specific events shaped every move they did and did not make. Our task is to acknowledge and explain that, and to account for what they would have been capable of imagining. In order to do that, we must simultaneously ground ourselves in history and open ourselves up to love stories.

Trying to write a story of love, one wrestles with the oppressive weight of loneliness on our histories. Sometimes we have clear evidence: Cooper wrote plaintively that she dreaded "treading the winepress alone."[17] And who wouldn't, even in the best of worlds? After the debacle with John Love, she gave full vent to her loneliness. Again, we are lucky she left us a poem, this time one she wrote during her years in

Missouri. Effectively exiled from the city she loved by censorious politicians and papers and petty educators, she penned "A Message":

> As the arc moves out to the circle,
> As pole cries aloud unto pole,
> As the brook rusheth on to its ocean,
> As soul leaps aloft to its soul,
> So I know—in the infinite spaces,
> In the infinite aeons of time,
> Somewhere my broken life traces
> The curve of its orbit sublime.
> Somewhere to the longing and yearning
> And hunger, satisfaction shall come.
> Somewhere I know I shall find you
> And my heart nestle sweetly at home.[18]

She wrote the poem out repeatedly. She typed it, and wrote it in cursive, and one time drew a little flower over it.[19] To ignore gestures like that, to imagine that her love poetry was not as important to understanding her as her political writings, impoverishes us. If this were a political commentary, we would not content ourselves with saying, "Oh, what matter who she intends?" So whom is she talking about? John Love? George Cooper? At the very least, this heartbreaking poem is about her, about how she understood herself. Lonely, aching, she wants back the home safety and the love she has lost. And perhaps she is reminding us that we should also be looking out for the shape of her heart.

> For every image of the past that is not recognized by the present as one of its own concerns threatens to disappear irretrievably. (The good tidings which the historian of the past brings with throbbing heart may be lost in a void the very moment he opens his mouth.)
>
> **—Walter Benjamin, "On the Concept of History"**

If I have learned that we must be skeptical of what our bodies might tell us about our subjects, if the unknowability of their social experiences potentially leaves their emotional and physical lives inaccessible to us, we must nevertheless talk about this. These are the matters that colored their days; their lives were as centered on the personal as ours are. Whether that personal was a richly rewarding emotional life or a lonely and unsatisfying one, it was central. This seems at once empathetic (of course they had human needs!) and presumptuous (why assume anything about the priorities of women who accomplished so much?).

Here, perhaps, is where my agenda most pressingly intrudes: I believe we all need these women to be models, not paragons. As unquestioned superheroines, they can offer us little to emulate; we might as well wish for a pocket full of thunderbolts, or the ability to fly.[20] But I don't believe these were Olympian figures, not even the greatly mythologized Anna Julia Cooper. These were flesh of our human flesh, embodied women. They were, by turns, lonely and loving and angry and adoring. Neither their history nor our needs can be served by failing to recognize that.

> I speak of our public history, and of our secret history, yours and mine.

> **—Octavio Paz, "I Speak of the City"**

Sometimes I wonder how this project might ever be done. I realize that I cannot construct the intimate life of my own grandmother, a woman with whom I have lived. Doubting, I wonder at how hazy the details of my own sexual history and emotional world have become. What have I done, or felt? And if I cannot remember even that, how might I hope to open a window onto the life of a woman so very far removed from me? One answer is to rely on history in the form of stories, the narratives of love and heartbreak that comprise a good deal of our subjects' affective history.[21]

Few genuinely intimate stories are available to us as we attempt to understand the minds of our characters. In addition to the creativity this history demands of my work in the archives, writing about intimacy and love holds my secondary source base up to new lights, some harsh and others rose-colored. Suddenly admirable histories seem inadequate; history itself becomes suspect. Is this the genre to which I should look to explain the hearts of my subjects? Can carefully researched accounts of changing mores account for individuals' loves and lonelinesses? Should I in fact be reading more novels, and if so, which ones? Shall I rule out Gabriel García Márquez (all that abandon in the violets— too bold by half), learn from Fyodor Dostoyevsky's strange unrequited loves and even stranger requited ones? Is Willa Cather calling me?

Or, if understanding depends on what we can imagine, perhaps more poetry is in order:

> ... poetry.
> It slips between yes and no,
> says what I keep silent,
> keeps silent what I say,
> dreams what I forget.[22]

Anna Julia Cooper, I must always remember, was a poet as well as a scholar. Can I write as creatively as she lived, trace her heart with my hands, craft a narrative that doesn't foreclose alternatives but rather forces us to entertain new ones?

Even historicization, crucial to a project of this nature, holds its own dangers. Cooper lived for well over a century. Born before Abraham Lincoln became president, she outlived John F. Kennedy; born before the Civil War, she died the year the Beatles played Shea Stadium. To see her simply as the product of the antebellum South, or as a Victorian woman, or even as a product of the Gilded Age diminishes the fact that she was politically and romantically active in the Progressive Era; that she raised children not only in the 1880s but also during the Harlem Renaissance; that she earned a Ph.D. as flappers were bobbing their hair, and then lived to see Rosie the Riveter and Rosa Parks. To write her history, and more specifically the history of her innermost heart, calls for constant questioning of her self-understanding.

Yet I must believe that this sort of project can be done using a historian's imagination—informed by literary studies, or psychology, but still essentially dependent on the tools of history. One of the most powerful we have is the ability to craft a narrative. My subjects understood themselves to be moving along a certain trajectory, and as a historian I should also be able to pick out that trajectory. It's not an easy project. My characters stubbornly resist the simple plot lines or motivations I might wish on them. I have to caution myself continually against the temptations of hindsight and presentism. Always, always, too-obvious answers and too-neat conclusions beckon.

In order to understand the story of her life, Cooper had to be able to order it somehow. As endlessly creative as the human heart may be, many of us rely on scripts to make sense of our histories. So perhaps the best way to get at Anna Julia Cooper's intimate thoughts is to see what we can about the possibilities available for her to imagine. How did she think a life might be lived? Here was a woman who had to write a script for her life even as she lived it. What, exactly, would be the story of a woman born into slavery who ended up at Oberlin College, and then Columbia University? She would have to make it up as she went along, but it would have to be plausible, because it would matter terribly for millions of other women and men.

Writing her story and the stories of other black foremothers, I sometimes feel that I come to know less and less about them. Ultimately, though, I have to believe that this unknowing is central to the project. Not knowing about them need not leave a void in our understanding. Rather, it may fill the space of their historical hearts with possibilities, and allow us to see that they lived not according to inimitable patterns, but in ways we can emulate, if only we can imagine them; just as they themselves imagined their lives, and then made them real.

8

WRITING FOR HISTORY: JOURNALISM, HISTORY, AND THE REVIVAL OF NARRATIVE

Jill Lepore

History is hot. And historians are seething.

In 2004, two of the *New York Times Book Review's* four nonfiction "best books of the year" were histories: a biography of a founding father (*Alexander Hamilton*, by journalist Ron Chernow) and the story of a founding moment (*Washington's Crossing*, by historian David Hackett Fischer). "We are living now in a new golden age of historical popularization," Princeton historian Sean Wilentz declared, despairingly, in a 2001 essay in the *New Republic*. "America Made Easy," Wilentz titled his piece, a review of David McCullough's best-selling biography of John Adams, in which he found time to attack PBS's *Jim Lehrer News Hour* ("for the . . . egregious advent of the 'presidential historian,' a hitherto unknown scholarly species"), Ken Burns's *Civil War* series ("crushingly sentimental and vacuous"), and Simon Schama's *New Yorker* essays and doorstop books ("erudite and jolly and empty") as so many "defections to the universe of entertainment." Taken together, McCullough's effusive praise of our second president, Michael Bechloss's suspiciously slick hair, Burns's cloying fiddle music, and Schama's dilettantism add up to the *American Heritage*-ization of history, a style Wilentz damns as "journalistic and sentimentally descriptive."

Once upon a time, Wilentz assures us, "American history was meant to rattle its readers, not to confirm them in their received myths and platitudes about America." But readers got tired of all that rattling. Beginning with *American Heritage*'s founding in 1954, that magazine and its imitators diverted readers from penetrating analysis by academic historians and investigative journalists. Today, no one reads scholarly monographs and "[t]he demand for blockbuster non-fiction historical epics has [even] defeated the best efforts of serious, iconoclastic journalists-turned-historians such as David Halberstam . . . and the late J. Anthony Lukas."

Historians will find much with to sympathize in Wilentz's argument. But are things really as bad as all that? Is all popular history simple, descriptive, entertaining, and rattle-free? Surely not. Journalists still write hard-hitting, best-selling books about history. Consider Toby Horwitz's Pulitzer Prize-winning *Confederates in the Attic*, or Adam Hochschild's *King Leopold's Ghost*. And there are even a few amazing books written by academic historians that are read by both Ph.D. students and PTA parents.

Yet Wilentz's "America Made Easy" voices a broader complaint about history for profit, one that's more difficult to refute: the History Channel, historical novels, and blockbuster biographers, he argues, have conspired to promote "the latest revival, under the banner of 'narrative,' of popular history as passive nostalgic spectacle."[1] Is he right? And if he is, and history has indeed become a "passive nostalgic spectacle," is narrative—and are journalists—to blame?

A BRIEF HISTORY OF HISTORY

Consider, first, the history of history. Here's the three-by-five index-card version. Ever since Eve first said "The serpent beguiled me," history has been told, and later written, as self-consciously crafted—even literary—stories about the past. Beginning in the eighteenth century, many forces conspired to turn history away from literature, and away from stories. Chief among them, in the nineteenth century, was professionalization. In 1884, the American Historical Association was founded—under the auspices of the American Social Science Association—to bring together "a great many scholars and educators who naturally take interest in the study of history and the working of causes on events." Its stated aims included "the discussion of methods"—not the discussion of prose style.

Then, beginning in the 1920s, and intensifying in the post-Sputnik era, a number of American and European professional historians began to insist that they could and should investigate historical "structures," not events, by employing scientific methods. To scientize the study of history, they quantified it. Especially in the 1960s and 1970s, historians counted things, from votes to Union dead to picnic tables. They used calculators. They made graphs. Their journal articles read like lab reports. Some of them wrote rattlingly good history; some of them wrote tripe. Most wrote books that, however important, wouldn't have kept you from your pajama-time P. G. Wodehouse chapter.

Yet, beginning in 1979—not coincidentally, the year the first Pulitzer Prize was awarded for feature writing—British historian Lawrence Stone heralded "the revival of narrative" in academic history writing. The story was back.

PREGNANT PRINCIPLES AND THICK NARRATIVES

Lawrence Stone has defined narrative as "the organization of material in a chronologically sequential order and focusing of the content into a single coherent story." (That this represented a departure from common practice should give you a sense of just how inhospitable to plot historical writing had become.) Unlike "structural" or "scientific" history, which is "analytical," narrative history is "descriptive." From most historians' point of view, to call a piece of writing "descriptive" is the worst kind of damnation. But, far from lamenting descriptive narratives, Stone celebrated them. Narrative history, he suggested, is by no means lacking in interpretation so long as it is "directed by some 'pregnant principle'" and "possesses a theme and an argument." What's more, historians writing stories care about writing; they "aspire to stylistic elegance, wit and aphorism. They are not content to throw words down on a page and let them lie there, with the view that, since history is a science, it needs no art to help it along."[2]

Stories with "pregnant principles" are hard to write, and especially difficult to write artfully. Many narrative histories written by academics take readers on sea-sickening sails that endlessly tack back and forth between story and argument. How to tell a story that does more than describe what happened is not immediately obvious, at least to academic historians. In a perceptive essay written in 1992, Cambridge University historian Peter Burke suggested that historians ought to borrow the anthropological notion of "thick description" ("a technique which interprets an alien culture through the precise and concrete description of particular practices and events") and write "thick narratives" that seamlessly integrate story and context. The problem for historians, Burke suggested, is "making a narrative thick enough to deal not only with the sequence of events and the conscious intentions of the actors in these events, but also with structures—institutions, modes of thought, and so on—whether these structures act as a brake on events or as an accelerator."[3]

In practice, since the 1980s "thick narratives" with "pregnant principles" have often taken the form of what historians somewhat ambivalently call "microhistories"—stories about a single, usually very ordinary person, place or event, that seek to reveal the society's broader structures. (Wilentz himself coauthored a microhistory in 1995, about an eccentric antebellum American evangelical, on the heels of Schama's 1991 microhistory about the gruesome murder of a Harvard Medical School doctor.) Most of the genre's best-known examples, like Carlo Ginzburg's *The Cheese and the Worms* (1980), Natalie Zemon Davis's *Return of Martin Guerre* (1984), and John Demos's *Unredeemed Captive* (1994), read like detective novels, in which historians gumshoe their way through the archives, seeking to understand the lives and motivations of compelling, if minor, historical actors. Their work rests on the central premise that ordinary lives, thickly described, illuminate culture best, a premise that has recently been taken to its logical—or preposterous—conclusion in Alain Corbin's 2001 study of an utterly obscure nineteenth-century French clog maker, "about whom nothing is known except for his entries in the civil registries," in the aptly titled *Life of an Unknown.*[4]

Telling small stories—writing microhistories—does not inevitably produce important scholarship. Just the opposite, alas, is far likelier. As Burke has warned, "the reduction in scale does not thicken a narrative by itself." Truth be told, microhistories have linked ordinary lives to grand historical themes with what can only be termed mixed success. When microhistories are good, they're breathtakingly brilliant; when they're bad, they're pretty much worthless.

IN COLD PROSE

Now consider the history of journalism. If twentieth-century academic historians turned their backs on storytelling in the early part of the century, only to return to it in the late 1970s, journalists trudged along a similar path. They scorned storytelling in favor of fact finding, and then changed their minds.

In the late-nineteenth- and early-twentieth-centuries, according to famed journalist Jon Franklin, the best American writers, reporters included, began their careers—and received their literary training—writing short stories. "The short story, in its heyday, was the universal school for writers," Franklin argues. The short story "demanded the utmost of the writer, both technically and artistically." It "served as the great eliminator of mediocre talent." When short story writers turned to reporting, they brought a drawerful of literary devices: an economy of prose, an eye for detail, an ear for dialogue, a keen sense of plot and resolution. But in the wake of World War II, when *Collier's* and the *Saturday Evening Post* closed shop, "the audience for quality short fiction all but vanished." In its place, Americans turned to short nonfiction. (And at just this moment, as Sean Wilentz reminds us, *American Heritage* was born.)

In the 1950s and 1960s, Franklin asserts, the quality of journalistic writing was devastated by the demise of the short-story apprenticeship. When journalism turned away from literature, newspaper and magazine writing lost its luster. "Nonfiction wasn't as good a training ground as the short story had been," Franklin points out, because it "emphasized subject over form and rewarded reporting skills at the expense of writing technique." But when *In Cold Blood* was published in 1965, it "melded the accuracy of nonfiction with the dramatic force of fiction" and "ushered in the new genre of nonfiction drama," a genre that today dwells in a "foggy frontier between journalism and literature."[5] It's not so foggy as to be unnavigable, however, and one of its most visible signposts was that first Pulitzer for feature writing, awarded in 1979 to Franklin himself.

What's to be gained by comparing the history of history with the history of journalism? A few critical insights: The revival of narrative in historical writing parallels the emergence of narrative journalism. And narrative history's most celebrated invention, the microhistory, bears a passing resemblance to narrative journalism's favored form, the nonfiction short story.

SHORT STORIES AND MICROHISTORIES

Microhistories and nonfiction short stories have a good deal in common. Both genres emerged in the 1970s in response to professional trends—especially prevalent in the 1950s—that valued accuracy and analysis more than literary flair. Microhistory and the much-vaunted "revival of narrative" in historical writing were responses to "structural" or quantitative history; narrative journalism and the nonfiction short story were reactions against investigative journalism's emphasis on fact finding over prose style.

These genres have stylistic similarities as well. Both microhistories and nonfiction short stories tend to concern themselves with the everyday experiences of ordinary people (what Franklin calls the "day in the life of a dogcatcher" and Corbin titles the "life of an unknown") as a means of offering broader cultural interpretations—moving from events to structures. Both genres self-consciously employ the techniques of dramatic fiction, including character development, plotting, and conflict resolution. Most microhistorians and narrative journalists aspire to write narratives thickened with the butter of detail and the flour of implication.

Microhistories and nonfiction short stories also fall prey to the same dangers. Burke considered small stories' greatest pitfall to be their tendency to "focus attention on the sensational." Both academics writing microhistories and journalists writing nonfiction short stories are drawn to the drama of murder trials, suicides, kidnapping, rapes, and other miscellaneous crimes and disasters.

It's easy to push this parallel too far. Crucial differences separate these two genres. Microhistories are not nonfiction short stories; they are micro in focus, not in length. Journalists sometimes write about the past, but most narrative journalism is not historical. Microhistories are intended to contribute to scholarly debate; nonfiction short stories are not.

Still, the similarities are intriguing, and they raise a key question: if narrative history and narrative journalism use similar devices, consider similar subjects, and are the consequences of related trends in politics and the arts, why, then, are historians and journalists not on better terms?

LONELY GENIUSES

"When a distinguished member of the school of 'new history' writes a narrative," Lawrence Stone has noted, "his friends tend to apologize for him, saying, 'Of course, he only did it for the money.'" It must be said that a great deal of the animosity so commonly expressed by academic historians toward popular history boils down to this: history books are selling like hotcakes, but journalists are making all the money.

To be fair, most historians have few intellectual objections to a rattling good history, so long as the story is told in the service of an argument. Often, it isn't. Burke has warned, "The revival of narrative may lead to a return to pure antiquarianism, to story-telling for its own sake." Or, worse still, for the sake of the nifty book advance.

Clearly, there's more than money at stake. Part of what grates academic historians is that many popular histories are, from their point of view, miscarried microhistories. That is, they tell a small story, but fail to use that story to interpret larger historical structures. At their worst, histories written by journalists are all headlines: they gesture at significance, but fail to demonstrate it.

These books also, from a historian's vantage point, appropriate the tools of microhistory not to recover the lives of ordinary men and women but to tell hackneyed stories about the famous, the celebrated, the world's great and lonely geniuses. They raise historians' hackles.

Far from thickly narrating a life, the worst popular histories also tend to rip people out of the past and stick them to the present, like so many Colorforms. These people from different places and times, they're just like us, only dead. Bad popular history, like bad historical novels and films, manages at once to exoticize the past (descriptions of clothes, hairstyles, houses, and the minutiae of daily life are always lovingly re-created) and to render familiar the people who lived in it. Fashions change, but complicated, historically specific ideas like sovereignty, progress, or childhood magically transcend history. Pocahontas might have worn a cloak of lice-infested deer hide, but she loved John Rolfe just like Laura loved Luke.

It's just this kind of writing that Sean Wilentz condemns as "passive nostalgic spectacle." But, to return to the question with which I began, is narrative—and are journalists—to blame?

THE BANNER OF NARRATIVE

When Wilentz decries "the latest revival, under the banner of 'narrative,' of popular history as passive nostalgic spectacle," he is regretting, in part, how the revival of narrative in the academy has legitimized popular historical writing: because both historians and journalists have embraced narrative, the line between scholarly and popular writing is now more difficult to discern. But Wilentz, like most historians, has failed to consider how the emergence of narrative journalism has contributed to the academic revival of narrative, and how much these two developments have in common. Truman Capote is not responsible for Ken Burns, David McCullough, and James McPherson, but he's not irrelevant either.

Much history today is written "under the banner of 'narrative.'" Does it inevitably render its readers passive? No, but perhaps it should. One kind of passivity—or maybe we should call it *enthrall-ment*—is a measure of success: readers can be nearly paralyzed by compelling stories, confidently told. In the hands of a good narrator, readers can be lulled into alternating states of wonder and agreement. What do you want your reader to say when reading your history? "Wow! Yes! Geez!"

Of course thoughtful history—or what Wilentz terms "serious history"—challenges its readers, too. What do you want your reader to say when you reveal your argument? "Wow, yes! But that means . . . ? And I wonder why they didn't . . . ?" And then you must have the answers at hand. Good writers anticipate how readers read. It's not that you want your readers to be struck dumb. You want to be able to predict what they'll say.

A HISTORY WORKSHOP

It's easier to see how this works—or doesn't work—by considering an example. In New York in 1741, more than 150 African slaves and 20 whites were accused of conspiring to burn the city and murder its inhabitants. After months of trials, 34 conspirators were hanged or burned at the stake, 15 more than were executed for witchcraft in Salem in 1692.[6]

Surely a historian can be forgiven the temptation of telling this story for its own sake. It burns with dramatic potential. But the story must have a point, a pregnant principle, an argument, or some corn starch. How might such a thickened narrative begin? Here are three possible opening scenes:[7]

Scene A

On the afternoon of Sunday, April 5, 1741, Abigail Earle was looking out the second-floor window of a house on Broadway when she saw "three negro men" coming up the street. As they passed the house, one of them, a slave named Quack, threw his hands in the air, laughed, and shouted, "*Fire, Fire, scorch, scorch!*" The next day, Quack was arrested. After three months in a dismal jail, he would confess to kissing a Bible at John Hughson's dockside tavern, pledging himself to a plot to burn the city. On July 18th he would be hanged at the gallows near the Battery.

But this counted for mercy: Quack was lucky not to be burned alive.

Scene B

Seventeen-year-old Sandy was a reluctant conspirator. One Sunday evening in February 1741, when he went out to get tea-water at Fresh Pond, in lower Manhattan, his friend Jack called him in to Gerardus Comfort's house. There he found twenty blacks, who got him drunk and attempted to swear him into a plot to burn the city. At first Sandy said no, but, threatened with knives and "afraid they would kill him," he promised to burn the Slip-Market. Back at the house of his master, Thomas Niblet, Sandy saw "Mr. Machado's negro wench called Diana" set fire to her master's house, next door. Diana "gave him four shillings to hold his tongue" and told him why she had done it: her mistress had taken "her own young child from her breast, and laid it in the cold [and] it froze to death." After which, the reluctant conspirator changed his mind. "God damn all the white people," he cursed the next morning at the water pump. "If he had it in his power, he would set them all on fire."

Scene C

On the morning of March 18, 1741, New York's governor hired a plumber to repair a leak in the gutter between his house and the chapel that stood next door, at the southernmost tip of Manhattan Island, next to the city's Fort George. The plumber came carrying a "fire-pot with coals to keep his soddering-iron hot," and set about his work. As he toiled at midday, a fierce wind blew from the harbor, sending sparks flying, right up to the house's wooden shingles. Within minutes, the roof was on fire, and the flames quickly spread to both the chapel and the fort. The chapel bells sounded the alarm but no eighteenth-century fire brigade could put out these flames. In little more than an hour, the governor's house "was burnt down to the ground, and the chapel and other buildings beyond human power of saving." Only a serendipitous early evening rain shower stopped the fire at the governor's stables. But the plumber's fire-pot was soon forgotten. At sundown, militia Captain Cornelius Van Horne beat a call to arms, and sent seventy soldiers to patrol the city until daylight, to prevent the city's general destruction by African arsonists.

Each of these scenes, I'd assert, could be called sensational, even (with less cause) sentimental, although decidedly not nostalgic. Each is descriptive, each narrative; each is a kind of spectacle. But each contains a different pregnant principle, the seeds of an argument that both engages readers interested in the history of slavery, and of New York, and contributes to long-standing debates among professional historians.

Abigail Earle's report of three slaves walking unescorted down Broadway in Scene A highlights the relative freedom of African slaves in eighteenth-century New York while the image of Quack's body hanging from the gallows concentrates the reader's attention on the brutality with which their alleged plotting was put down. Imagine that the point of telling this story is to argue that urban slavery is inherently unstable, an argument that introduces the even broader claim that the 1741 New York slave "conspiracy" spelled the end of slavery in the North, a generation before the rhetoric of the American Revolution effected its legal abolition. Scene A doesn't make this claim, but it sets it up.

Sandy's conversion to the cause of the conspiracy, traced in Scene B, urges the reader to wrestle with the fundamental ferocity of chattel slavery, symbolized by the story of Diana's putting her newborn baby out to freeze to death. This scene introduces themes to be developed in an argument that will reveal the inevitability of slave plotting in a city dotted with central gathering places—the water pump, Comfort's tavern, the Slip-Market—in which black men and women congregate and discuss their grievances. Although an organized, transatlantic antislavery movement is often dated to the 1740s, historians have never considered slaves to be an active part of this movement, or even, really, aware of its existence. Sandy's politicization foreshadows an argument that ideas of private property ownership—at base, of the possession of one's own body—pervaded the cultural world of slaves in mid-eighteenth-century New York.

Finally, beginning the story of the New York conspiracy with the plumber's soldering iron, in Scene C, stakes out a radically different position: it discredits the whole idea of a plot to burn the city by insisting that the fire at Fort George was purely accidental. Pointing to the military patrol serves to introduce the extravagance of white New Yorkers' reaction to what, to them, was the worst form of terrorism, fire, and their unthinking suspicion of the African population (at the time, one-fifth of the city's inhabitants).

Three scenes, three stories, three arguments. Whether these scenes work depends, of course, on what comes next. If they are to be more than stories for their own sake, they must connect these historical events to historical structures: the nature of urban slavery, the transatlantic antislavery movement, Enlightenment theories of racial difference. My point is that storytelling is not a necessary evil in the writing of history; it's a necessary good. Using stories to make historical arguments makes sense. A writer who wants to can pummel his reader into passivity, but a writer who wants to challenge his reader betters his odds of success by telling a story.

Three scenes, three stories, three arguments. And maybe one of these stories rattles.

9

"WE SHOULD GROW TOO FOND OF IT": WHY WE LOVE THE CIVIL WAR[1]

Drew Gilpin Faust

"If war were not so terrible," Robert E. Lee observed as he watched the slaughter at Fredericksburg, "we should grow too fond of it." Lee's remark, uttered in the very midst of battle's horror and chaos, may be his most quoted—and misquoted—statement. His exact words are in some dispute, and it seems unlikely we shall ever be able to be certain of precisely what he said to James Longstreet on December 13, 1862. But in every rendition of the quotation, the contradiction between war's attraction and its horror remains at the heart. War is terrible and yet we love it; we need to witness the worst of its destruction in order not to love it even more. And both because and in spite of its terror, we must calibrate our feelings to ensure enough, but not too much, fondness. It is Lee's succinct, surprising, and almost poetic expression of a too often unacknowledged truth about war that has made this statement so quotable. Lee, the romantic hero of his own time and the marble man of ages that followed, displays here a complexity, an ambivalence, a capacity for irony that suggest cracks in the marble. His observation seems to reach beyond his era and its sensibilities into our own.[2]

Lee was not alone among his contemporaries in articulating a fondness for war, though few had his sense of irony. Many Americans North and South looked forward to battle in 1861, anticipating a stage on which to perform deeds appropriate to a Romantic age but believing, too, that war would be salutary for both the nation and its citizens. Judah P. Benjamin, attorney general of the new Confederacy, reassured a New Orleans crowd in the winter of 1861 that war was far from an "unmixed evil," for it would "stimulate into active development the nobler impulses and more elevated sentiments which else had remained torpid in our souls." *DeBow's Review* anticipated from war "a sublime and awful beauty—a fearful and terrible loveliness—that atones in deeds of high enterprise and acts of heroic valor for the carnage, the desolation, the slaughter." Others were not so rash in their estimates of the likely balance between glory and horror yet nevertheless found in the coming of war welcome opportunity for self-definition and fulfillment. In the North, Henry Lee Higginson later looked back on his hopes for the conflict: "I always did long for some such war, and it came in the nick of time for me."[3]

Northerners and Southerners alike saw in imminent war the possibility for a cleansing corrective to the greed and corruption into which Americans had fallen. Historian Francis Parkman wrote to the *Boston Advertiser* that American society had been "cramped and vitiated" by "too exclusive a pursuit of material success," but he was certain that through war the nation would be "clarified and pure in a renewed and strengthened life." In a June 1861 editorial, the *Richmond Enquirer* rhapsodized that "a season of war . . . calls out new ideas and kindles new and more elevated emotions and sentiments. It appeals to all that is noble in the soul . . . it revives the slumbering emotions of patriotism, with all their generous joys. It restores the general brotherhood. It destroys selfishness. It begets the spirit of self sacrifice. It gives to sufferers a portion of that ecstasy which martyrs feel." The paper assured its readers that "many virtues will glow and brighten in . . . [war's] path, like fragrant flowers in the wilderness." But it would not be fragrant flowers that Virginians would soon be finding in the Wilderness.[4]

Often war's expected transformations were framed in religious terms—as processes of divine purification resulting from the sacrifices required by war. Sermons in the North and the South hailed war's chastening rod. More secular observers welcomed war's imposition of discipline and even subordination into a society disrupted by undue egalitarianism, selfishness, and disorder.[5]

The realities of battlefield slaughter and enormous death tolls did not destroy this enthusiasm for war's purposes. Paeans to war did not cease as the conflict grew more intense and more terrible. Fought in

April 1862, Shiloh marked a new departure in warfare, a level of death and destruction previously unknown and unimagined. Yet Charles Eliot Norton responded to the carnage by writing, "I can hardly help wishing that the war might go on and on till it has brought suffering and sorrow enough to quicken our consciences and cleanse our hearts." Great battles were believed to be occasions and sites for profound reflection and insight, and Northerners and Southerners alike were eager to learn, to borrow the title of a *Richmond Enquirer* editorial, "What War Should Teach Us."[6]

Civilians rushed to Antietam or Gettysburg not only to care for the wounded or to collect relics but also to experience the lessons that only a battlefield could convey. A Union quartermaster estimated that as many as 5,000 people a day swarmed into Gettysburg in the battle's immediate aftermath. Many soldiers regarded these civilians with contempt, seeing their presence as a hindrance to providing care for the injured and graves for the dead. War correspondent Sylvanus Cadwallader described "greedy sight seers . . . there to gratify their morbid curiosity," and *Leslie's Illustrated News* published an almost cartoonlike engraving of "Maryland and Pennsylvania Farmers Visiting the Battlefield of Antietam while the National Troops Were Burying the Dead and Carrying off the Wounded." A gruesome pile of tangled bodies fills the left foreground of the engraving; buzzards fly overhead; the Army burial detail labors in the background while four well-dressed civilians, including a woman and a child, gape at the repulsive sight. Presumably these sightseers are being relieved of their Romantic fascination with war.[7]

But many civilians continued to be attracted by war's power and to search avidly for its lessons and meaning. After kissing a dying soldier at Malvern Hill, Reverend E. L. Locke explained his hope "that we who are spectators might be the truer and braver for what we had seen." On the Northern homefront Mary Percy was eager to "talk with one who has been in a real bona fide fight. I want him to tell me what the sensations are." Walt Whitman shared her desire to understand combat and longed "to be present at a first class battle." His hospital work thrilled him—not so much because of the service he was able to render, but, as he explained it, because the wounded opened "a new world somehow to me, giving closer insights . . . exploring deeper mines—than any yet, showing our humanity . . . tried by terrible, fearfulest tests, probed deepest, the living soul's, the body's tragedies, bursting the petty bonds of art." The war years, he later observed, brought the "greatest privilege and satisfaction" because they "brought out . . . undream'd of depths of emotion." War enabled Whitman, and many others, to achieve that most desired of goals in this Romantic age: an enhanced ability to feel.[8]

Civilians, as Charles Royster has noted, sought a "vicarious war," but many soldiers rejoiced in war as well, even after the destructiveness and horror of Civil War battle became evident. For all the slaughter at Shiloh, one Iowa soldier remarked, "I would not have missed this for any consideration." And Joshua Lawrence Chamberlain confessed just a few weeks after the disastrous and bloody Northern defeat at Fredericksburg that he had never felt so well or so truly alive. Henry James admitted to profound envy of his younger soldier brother Wilky, even after he was severely wounded at Fort Wagner. Apparently medically unfit for service himself, Henry resented that "this soft companion of my childhood should have such romantic chances and should have mastered . . . such mysteries." In the military both Wilky and a second brother, Robertson, had gained "wondrous opportunity of vision." James feared "they would prove to have had the time of their lives." Even Ambrose Bierce, whose postbellum short stories so vividly portray the Civil War's horrors, understood war's attractions all too well. The lure of war, he wrote, its bugle call, "goes to the heart as wine . . . . Who that has heard its call to him above the grumble of the great guns can forget the wild intoxication of its music?"[9]

Historians have shared this intoxication with war. War has been perhaps history's most popular subject, and recent years have only seen that interest intensify. Within the American field this fondness for war has manifested itself most dramatically in the dedication of so many historians to Civil War subjects. Many of us have chosen to devote our professional lives to exploring the Civil War, identifying it as a topic that interests us above all others. Certainly a desire to study war is different from a passion to fight it, but both acknowledge its attraction, its fascination, its power, and its importance.

Why do historians love the Civil War? Why has the Civil War come to be one of the liveliest fields in American history? We are part of a long tradition of writing about the war. More than 60,000 volumes of Civil War history had appeared by the end of the twentieth century, more than a book a day since Appomattox. But we represent a more recent phenomenon as well—one that has been characterized as an explosion of Civil War scholarship—what has been called a Civil War "industry," and a "new Civil War history."[10]

How can we more precisely describe this explosion, this new and sizeable "wave" of Civil War studies? What are the factors that have produced this recent volume of writing? And what are the new directions and perspectives that have made the Civil War so attractive a subject to the current generation of scholars? How should we understand this growing fondness for the Civil War? [11]

Many commentators have dated the beginning of the recent dramatic expansion of interest in Civil War history to the 1988 publication and astonishing popular success of James M. McPherson's *Battle Cry of Freedom*. Oxford University Press planned a very respectable initial print run for *Battle Cry* of 20,000 books. In what was, McPherson says, a "BIG (though of course pleasant) surprise" to both author and publisher, it became a *New York Times* hardcover best-seller for sixteen weeks, won the Pulitzer Prize, and has ultimately sold more than 600,000 copies. Successfully appealing both to professional historians and to a wider popular audience of Civil War enthusiasts, *Battle Cry* demonstrated that scholarship produced in the academy could indeed reach beyond its walls. The inspiring—as well as venal—hope for such a wide readership riveted historians' attention on *Battle Cry* as a publishing event and on the Civil War as a subject that might bring attention, acclaim, and even riches. But in fact, McPherson's book was the beneficiary rather than the cause of an already increasing interest in the Civil War. [12]

In an effort better to understand the dimensions of the much noted recent growth in Civil War history, I undertook a survey of Civil War books reviewed since 1976 in the *Journal of Southern History*, which, despite its title, considers studies on both Northern and Southern aspects of the conflict. The *JSH* includes a broader representation of general-interest Civil War books than are reviewed by either the *Journal of American History* or the *American Historical Review*, yet it draws the line at works of such specialized focus as to address no significant interpretive or intellectual questions.

In 1976 the *JSH* reviewed 13 Civil War books. In 2002 it reviewed 66. That is a fivefold increase. How did we get from there to here? From 1976 through 1987 the numbers average 13 a year, varying between a low of 7 in 1980 to a high of 21 in 1982. We should remember the idiosyncrasies of academic reviewing, especially the lag of about a year between publication date and published review. But through these 12 years, the numbers are quite consistent. Then in 1989 there is a dramatic rise—to 27 books. This is, in fact, the year that *Battle Cry* was reviewed, suggesting, intriguingly, that McPherson's book was part of an already emerging phenomenon. For 4 years the number of books hovers at this level, and then we see a second significant increase, in 1993, to 45 books. Over the next decade the average number per year is 48, though the two most recent years, with totals of 64 and 66, may represent the beginning of a third, still higher, phase.

The jump in 1993 from an average in the preceding 4 years of 28 books to an average of 45 books over the next 10 years (an increase of more than 60 percent) may well be attributable to the extraordinary reception and impact of Ken Burns's *The Civil War.* This 11-hour series broke television records in the fall of 1990 when it attracted an audience of 14 million. By the end of the decade more than 40 million Americans had watched one or more episodes. Burns has himself offered an explanation of why Americans loved his *Civil War.* The conflict, he explained, "continues to speak to central questions of our present time." He noted "an imperial presidency, a growing feminist movement . . . an ever present civil rights question . . . greedy Wall Street speculators who stole millions trading on inside information . . . unscrupulous military contractors . . . new weapons capable of mass destruction" as Civil War-era issues with particular resonance for contemporary Americans.[13]

Writers before Burns had found evidence in the Civil War era of what historians Peter Parish and Adam I. P. Smith have called the "increasingly recognizable shape of modern America." We see ourselves and our concerns reflected in this history. Yet the war intrigues us not simply because we identify with its central issues, not just because it seems curiously modern. We have found in it, as David Montgomery has explained, "so critical a moment in the formation of the world in which we live that it compels us to contemplate the most basic features and values of modern society." The war, he suggests, has in fact made us, has set the agenda for the world we now inhabit. We look to the war for our origins.[14]

But this sense of the war, embraced and represented by Burns, was also far from new with him, even if he was the first to offer it so compellingly in the magical medium of television. Historians and writers had long been captivated by the war as the site and reason for the emergence of modern America, even though they might have disagreed about which attributes of this modernity to stress: the establishment of a centralized nation-state, the creation of a vigorous industrial economy, the forging of new meanings for freedom and citizenship of and by and for the people.

Was there a reason in the late 1980s and early 1990s that what we might call a chronic interest in the Civil War became acute? The Gulf War of 1991 was, of course, a significant factor, for Burns's series aired during a fall of anticipations and anxieties about the outbreak of war.

The contemporary relevance of Civil War questions was forcefully underscored by the coincidence of the release of Burns's documentary with a real-life military drama. President George H. W. Bush, Colin Powell, and even General Norman Schwarzkopf at his post in Saudi Arabia watched the series as they contemplated their own decisions about the conflict they inaugurated in January 1991. Burns's depiction of the Civil War's terrible casualties reportedly reinforced their commitment to minimize American deaths as they developed their strategic plans. [15]

Operation Desert Storm, with its quick, seemingly easy, and, in U.S. terms, almost bloodless victory, brought war back into fashion in America. The bitterness that had followed Vietnam and the rejection of war as an effective instrument of national policy had been challenged throughout the Reagan years. But the slow rehabilitation of war in the course of the 1980s culminated in 1991's dramatic victory. Growing interest in the Civil War in the late 1980s reflected gradually changing American attitudes about military action, attitudes further and decisively affected by the conjunction in the fall of 1990 and the winter of 1991 of Ken Burns's compelling visual rendition of the conflict and with George H. W. Bush's splendid little war.

Historians who recognized war as back in fashion in Reagan-Bush America did not necessarily celebrate its return, just as many scholars vehemently criticized the overwhelming military focus of the Burns's documentary. A considerable proportion of the scholars who began to direct their attention to the Civil War were children of the Vietnam era, individuals struck by the changed political atmosphere in the 1980s, individuals who had lived through a period when war was at the heart of American public life and discourse in the late 1960s and 1970s, individuals who wanted to understand the historic roots of America's relationship with war as they now witnessed its late-century return to respectability. And although their critical perspective sharply differentiated them from a wider public that gloried in the success of Desert Storm and relished the elegiac seriousness of Ken Burns's soldier-patriots, these scholars saw in Civil War history the possibility of reaching across this divide not only to sell books but also to add important considerations to wider American public discourse. Loving the Civil War, we must not forget, has created some strange bedfellows.

The Civil War created strange bedfellows within the historical profession as well. Many academics who discovered an awakening interest in the Civil War in the late 1980s and early 1990s came to the subject with historical training and experience quite different from that of the military and political historians who had overwhelmingly dominated the literature. "Never before," wrote James McPherson and William Cooper looking back in 1998, "have so many scholars of the war ranged so widely over so many fields." If Maris Vinovskis worried in 1989 that social historians had lost the Civil War, they had by the end of the next decade certainly found it, connecting home and battle fronts and situating the Civil War battlefield decisively in the larger context of nineteenth-century American life. Three developments seem to me of particular note: the introduction of social history, with particular emphasis on the life and importance of the common soldier, into study of the Civil War military; the use of the community study as a window into the interplay of war's myriad effects and actors; and the growing interest in the experience of women and of African Americans.[16]

Significantly, this new social history—this invasion into Civil War territory by social historians, women's historians, African-American historians—has done little to diminish the proportional strength of military history. As the number of social histories of the war has increased, so too has the number of military studies. Military history made up 57 percent of titles in 1988 and 69 percent of titles in 2002. On average over that fifteen-year period, 65 percent of titles were in military history. To some degree the military history of 2002 represented a changed and broadened approach, as it considered civilians in collections of essays on particular battles or explored the life of the common soldier as well as that of the general or, in the words of the editors of one series on Great Campaigns, looked "beyond the battlefield and headquarters tent." But the rapprochement of Civil War military history with social and cultural concerns is far from complete; audiences remain largely separate and segmented. The "crossover" success of Battle Cry remains the exception rather than the rule.[17]

Yet social historians have been attracted to the war by some of the same elements that engage military scholars. The Civil War offers an authenticity and intensity of experience that can rivet both researcher and reader; the war serves as a moment of truth, a moment when individuals—be they soldiers or civilians—have to define their deeply held priorities and act on them. War is a crucible that produces unsurpassed revelations about the essence of historical actors and their worlds. James McPherson has described his work with the papers of more than a thousand soldiers: "From such writings I have come to know these men better than I know most of my living acquaintances, for in their personal letters written in a time of crisis that might end their lives at any moment they revealed more of themselves than we do in our normal everyday lives." War can exact from individuals just what historians hope to find: expressions of their truest selves. We follow as historians in the footsteps of many of our century's—and our civilization's—greatest writers. As Ernest Hemingway once explained to F. Scott Fitzgerald, who enlisted too late for any significant World War I experience, "The reason you are so sore you missed the war is because war is the best subject of all. It groups the maximum of material and speeds up the action and brings out all sorts of stuff that normally you have to wait a lifetime to get." No wonder we love to study war. [18]

The new Civil War historians have found in the war years an extraordinarily rich field for exploration of many of the approaches and issues that had become central to professional historical practice since the 1970s. Because the war had been almost exclusively the domain of military historians, it represented an almost untapped resource for social and cultural historians. The war was, in addition, a historical moment that was extraordinarily well documented, for mid-nineteenth-century Americans were highly literate; soldiers' letters were uncensored; and expanding government and military bureaucracies North and South accumulated vast records of both public and private lives. Historians confronted a combination of unstudied questions and vast documentation as they recognized the opportunity to pursue previously neglected issues central to the revolution the 1970s and 1980s had brought to the historical enterprise.

Historians' work in uncovering and documenting the lives of groups once labeled "inarticulate"—workers, slaves, women—had embodied a fundamental commitment to giving these new subjects of historical inquiry both voice and agency. We learned in the 1970s and 1980s how workers' actions shaped economic growth, how slaves manipulated and resisted their masters, how women used voluntary associations to control men in domains of life from sexuality to party politics. The Civil War, with its decisive events in the realms of both of battle and of national policy, with its clearly defined moments of truth, offered unparalleled opportunity to explore, document, and highlight these examples of human agency. Military and political historians have long loved war because they could demonstrate the critically important actions of generals and politicians. As Mark Grimsley has observed, "Battles alter history. They decide things." Now social historians would seize the same opportunity to demonstrate far more dramatically than had been possible in their studies of lengthy social movements and processes that the actions of the so-called inarticulate mattered.[19]

Traditional Civil War historians have long been caught up in questions of causation: Why did the Civil War happen? Why did the North win? Why did the South lose? Why was slavery overturned? New Civil War historians directly confronted these conventional problems, accepting their predecessors' definition of the terms of engagement, lured by their fascination with issues of agency to fight on enemy ground. In the new Civil War history homefront rivaled battlefront as the decisive factor in war's outcome; common soldiers, rather than generals became the critical military factors in triumph or defeat; women undermined the stability of slavery and the level of civilian morale and contributed to Southern defeat or, conversely, struggled both at home and in military disguise to ensure victory. Perhaps most notably, slaves freed themselves. This is not the time or place to evaluate the legitimacy of these interpretations. At a minimum, I think we would agree that they have sparked vigorous and constructive debate that has enriched and broadened Civil War historiography. But I describe them here with the purpose of demonstrating how social historians melded their agendas with the traditional preoccupations of the Civil War field; they recognized and used the Civil War as a site to explore concerns that had been at the heart of the revolutions in methods and subject matter of the 1970s. And they used the Civil War to engage social history with event as well as process and to show how it became political and even military in its effects. The Civil War offered social historians the chance to capture new territory. But in this imperial gesture, they ironically largely accepted the prevailing framework of Civil War studies, refining traditional questions, especially those of causation, rather than posing new ones. The war as moment of truth, as occasion for decisive action, as laboratory for agency—even for heroism—was a war both old and new Civil War historians could love. [20]

But to describe the movement by social historians into the Civil War as just a calculated strategy to extend domain and audience is to miss a critical component of the phenomenon. The new Civil War historians have been caught up, like their predecessors, in the drama of the conflict, in the powerful human stories that stand apart from the analytic and interpretive goals of the historian as social scientist. Ken Burns has described himself as above all "a historian of emotions." Emotion, he has said, "is the great glue of history." Certainly it was the glue and the appeal of his television narrative. The American public loved *The Civil War* not primarily because it dealt with constitutional or political or racial or social questions that matter today, but because it was about individual human beings whose faces we could see, whose words we could hear, as they confronted war's challenges. The presence, the threat, even the likelihood of death imposes a narrative structure and thrust on Civil War stories. The exercise of agency is always inflected by this unavoidable question; decisions are quite literally matters of life and death. The presence of such risks places the lives that interest us on a plane of enhanced meaning and value, for life itself has become the issue and cannot be taken for granted. Death offers every chronicler of war a natural narrative shape, an implicit climax for every story, a structured struggle for every tale.[21]

And the accumulations of these many narratives, these thousands and thousands of deaths into the Civil War's massive death toll, have given the conflict, as James McPherson has written, a "horrifying but hypnotic fascination," a fascination I would suggest is almost pornographic in its combination of thrill and terror. We are in some sense not so different from those New Yorkers who in 1862 crowded in to see Mathew Brady's photographs of the Antietam dead, photographs fresh from the front offering the Northern public—as they still offer us—a vicarious taste of war. We are not, as Lee reminds us, the first Americans to grow fond of the Civil War. We are both moved by the details of war's suffering and terror and captivated by the unsurpassed insight war offers into the fundamental assumptions and values of historical actors. Despite our dispassionate, professional, analytic stance, we have not remained untouched by war's elemental attractions and its emotional and sentimental fascinations. We count on these allures to build a sizeable audience for our books. In both the reality and irony of our fondness for war, we are not so unlike the Civil War generation we study.[22]

As America stood on the brink of our most recent war with Iraq, journalist Chris Hedges published a best-selling book warning of war's seductive power, its addictiveness. War, he explained, simplifies and focuses life; it offers purpose and thus exhilarates and intoxicates; it is, in the words of Hedges's title, a "force that gives us meaning." And humans crave meaning as much as life itself. Caught in war's allure, we ignore its destructiveness—not just of others but of ourselves.[23]

The love affair with war Hedges describes has deep roots in history. He invokes examples from classical Greece, from Shakespeare, as well as from wars of our own time, just as I have been exploring the seductions of America's Civil War. Hedges offers no real solution to the problem he describes. He simply ends his book with calls for love, for Eros in face of Thanatos. And indeed, as his book climbed the best-seller list, the United States turned its love of war into the invasion of Iraq, endeavoring to transform the uncertainty of fighting a terrorist enemy without a face or location into a conflict with a purposeful, coherent, and understandable structure—with a comprehensible narrative.

In the United States's need to respond to terrorism with war, we can see a key element of war's appeal. War is not random, shapeless violence. It is a human, a cultural *construction*, an "invention," as Margaret Mead once described it, that imposes an order, a purpose, and indeed a control on violence. Through its implicit and explicit conventions, through its rules, war limits and structures its violence; it imbues violence with a justification, a trajectory, and a purpose. The United States sought a war through which to respond to terrorism—even a war against an enemy who had no relationship to the September 11 terrorist acts would do—because the nation required the sense of meaning, intention, and goal-directedness, the lure of efficacy that war promises; the control that terrorism obliterates. The nation needed the sense of agency that operates within the structure of narrative provided by war.

War is defined and framed as a story, with a plot that imbues its actors with purpose and moves toward victory for one or another side. This is why it provides the satisfaction of meaning to its participants; this is why, too, it offers such a natural attraction to writers and historians. Yet just as we need war, because in Hemingway's words, it is "the best subject of all," so in some sense war needs us. Writers and historians are critical to defining and elaborating the narratives that differentiate war from purposeless violence, the stories that explain, contextualize, construct, order, and rationalize—eliding from one to the other meaning of that word—what we call war. Are we then simply another part of the dangerous phenomenon Hedges has described? In writing about war, even against war, do we nevertheless reinforce its attraction and affirm its meaning? "When we write about warfare," Hedges warns, "the prurient fascination usually rises up to defeat the message." What, indeed, is the message that our historiography conveys? "Is there," as Susan Sontag has asked, "an antidote to the perennial seductiveness of war?" Are we as historians part of the problem or part of the solution?[24] Attracted by the potential narrative coherence of war, we also create and reinforce it. Out of historians' war stories—from Thucydides onward—we have fashioned war's seeming rationality and helped to define its meaning. Have we in so doing contributed to its allure?

Historian George Mosse once warned, "We must never lose our horror, never try to integrate war and its consequences into our longing for the sacred. . . . [I]f we confront mass death naked, stripped of all myth, we may have slightly more chance to avoid making the devil's pact" with war. But the effort to retain our horror is immensely aided by our recognition and acknowledgment of war's attractions. The complexity of irony disrupts myth, undermines unified narrative and unexamined purpose, questions meaning. [25]

When we recognize, like Robert E. Lee, that war is both terrible and alluring, we may move both ourselves and our history to a different place. We separate ourselves from war's myths through irony and open ourselves to its contradictions. Yet if we cannot understand why we love it, we cannot comprehend and explain why it has seduced so many others. In acknowledging its attraction we diminish its power. Perhaps we can free ourselves to construct a different sort of narrative about its meaning. But I am not sure.

It was Vietnam that gave many of us both the motivation and the ability to look critically at war, to be both fascinated and repelled. Michael Herr's brilliant book *Dispatches* is unflinching in its portrait of the horror and the purposeless of this war. It is a book, significantly, without a narrative, a book of glimpses, a book as chaotic as war itself. He had left, as the language of the time had it, "the world," to live in a surreal space beyond the possibility of understanding. Yet he returns at the end—"Back in the World"—with an observation that uncannily echoes Robert E. Lee and even Henry James: Herr finds himself "like everyone else who has been through a war: changed, enlarged and . . . incomplete. . . . coming to miss the life so acutely. . . . A few extreme cases felt that the experience there had been a glorious one, while most of us felt that it had been merely wonderful. I think that Vietnam was what we had instead of happy childhoods."[26]

Michael Herr was, like us, a writer of war. He was not a soldier; his tour in Vietnam was as a journalist. He wrote *Dispatches*, perhaps the best book to come out of that far-from-unwritten war, and he has hardly been heard of since. War was his only subject. He loved it and he knew it was terrible, and in that lay the power of his prose. Without war he disappeared. [27]

War made Michael Herr possible; it gave him a voice. But the voices of writers and storytellers have also made war possible from ancient times to the present day. I have written elsewhere about the role of war stories in mobilizing both men and women for war. [28] Seductive tales of glory, honor, sacrifice provide one means of making war possible.

But there is another more complex way as well, one that does not depend on an idealization or romanticization of war. War is, by its very definition, a story. War imposes an orderly narrative on what without its definition of purpose and structure would be simply violence. We as writers create that story; we remember that story; we provide the narrative that by its very existence defines war's purpose and meaning. We love war because of these stories. But we should ask ourselves how in the construction of war's stories we may be helping to construct war itself. "War is a force that gives us meaning." But what do we and our writings give to war?

Section III

The Politics of Writing

10

OUR SILENCES WILL HURT US: JOURNALISTIC WRITING IN A WOMEN'S PRISON

Eleanor M. Novek and Rebecca Sanford

INTRODUCTION

The act of writing has special significance in prison. For people who are incarcerated, writing can be a way to overcome the suffocating sense of obliteration they feel when the iron gates clang shut behind them. In a women's prison, many inmates turn to some form of expressive writing, some for the first time in their lives. Their writing serves many purposes, helping the authors maintain a sense of identity as well as a connection to others under soul-destroying conditions.

In 2001, the authors of this essay began teaching journalism classes in the minimum- and maximum-security wings of a state prison for women in the northeastern United States. As communication professors and researchers, we initiated this project in the tradition of feminist and social justice research, "the engagement with and advocacy for those in our society who are economically, socially, politically and/or culturally under-resourced" (Frey et al., 1996, 110). The project's goal was to enable incarcerated women to develop the communicative skills necessary to create an inmate newspaper. We hoped the participants in the journalism classes would be able to use writing to claim a voice and empower themselves to publish a newspaper. Throughout history,

Linda Steiner observes, women have established their own forms of independent media to "articulate and dramatize their emerging interests, to nourish and defend an identity that imbues their lives with meaning" (1992, 121).

For the last three years, participants in this project have produced a newspaper about once a month. The publication enables the writings of inmates to be shared with the prison's constituents—the inmate population, corrections officers, staff, and administrators. As this essay will illustrate, the writing done by the women in this project has allowed them to create a sense of personal worth in a hostile environment, and has offered a mechanism for the supportive sharing of meaning in a system that otherwise subjugates and silences prisoners.

When we learned that we would be speaking about the prison journalism project at the Why We Write conference at Columbia University in March 2003, we asked the women in our journalism classes to describe, in writing, how they would like us to represent them at the conference. One wrote that we should "emphasize the fact that we are women who may have made some serious mistakes but are not the monsters the media and society put us out to be. We are mothers, sisters, daughters and women." This will be our goal here. In addition, to protect confidentiality, the names of the women and the institution where the newspaper project takes place are not used in this essay.

PRISON WRITING IN CONTEXT

One of the more troubling social phenomena to occur over the last several decades is the dynamic growth of the nation's incarceration rate. Michel Foucault has called the prison "a detestable solution" (1979, 232), generating disquiet and disagreement in societies that employ it. Prisons are useless at stopping criminality, he notes, arguing that they are, in fact, responsible for institutionalizing and reproducing violence. Depending upon their political climates, societies have sometimes viewed the prison as an engine of discipline for the punishment of criminals, while at other times they have seen the penitentiary as a meditative cloister for the rehabilitation of lawbreakers.

Over the past three decades, U.S. public policy has favored increasingly tougher sentencing laws, more jails, harsher punishment, and more executions, leading to a period of unprecedented growth in the nation's prison system. Thus, in the last twenty years, the number of

Americans in prison has tripled; the United States now imprisons more of its citizens per capita than any other country in the world (Sentencing Project, 2001). In mid-2003, an estimated 2.1 million men and women were serving sentences in jails or prisons, and another 4.8 million were on probation or parole (Glaze and Palla, 2004).

In the same period, the female population of the U.S. corrections system doubled. Last year the number of women incarcerated in state or federal prisons reached an all-time high of 100,102 (Harrison and Karberg, 2004). Most of the women in prison are over the age of thirty, have at least a high school diploma or general eqivalency diploma, and are women of color; most are single mothers of young children and have grown up in single-parent households themselves (Pollock, 2002). More than 40 percent report a history of physical or sexual abuse (Girshick, 1999), and more than 25 percent are mentally ill (Human Rights Watch, 2003).

Educational disadvantage, drug and alcohol addiction, and mental illness are pervasive among the incarcerated population. Yet our prisons devote only a minuscule amount of their budgets to education, vocational training, or treatment (Sentencing Project, 2001). These disturbing trends create alarming conditions for millions of incarcerated Americans, their families, and their communities.

When the women in the journalism classes were imprisoned, they were thrust into a social system that isolated them from their loved ones and severely suppressed their communication with the outside world. At this facility, family visits are harshly restricted and closely supervised, with conversation and touch strictly limited and body searches taking place before and after the meetings. Telephone calls may last only fifteen minutes, must be made collect, and may be monitored. All incoming mail to prisoners—letters, publications, and packages—is opened and inspected; outgoing mail may also be read. Prisoners have no access to e-mail or the Internet. Faced with so many hurdles, family contact may decline or cease altogether when a woman is serving a lengthy sentence.

Communication inside these prison walls is also tightly circumscribed. To avoid disciplinary actions, inmates must be subservient when interacting with the prison hierarchy, staff members and correction officers. Communication between prisoners here is closely regulated, too; women who live in different residence halls may not freely associate, and the populations of the minimum- and maximum-security wings may not communicate with each other except through the mail. Access to the prison's daily newspapers, magazines, books, and television may be rationed. Library hours are brief, and library collections are minuscule, tattered, and out-of-date.

With daily communication so constrained, is it any wonder that inmates turn to writing to preserve their sense of self and connections to others? In the articles, essays, and poems published in the prison newspaper, women reclaim their voices, constructing identities from fragments of their pasts and hopes for their futures. The process is not without complications; the writers do not write freely, but act within a constricted set of rules established and perpetuated by the prison administration and by us, the professors offering the journalism classes. Some writers experience direct administrative expurgation, while others may self-censor, avoiding certain topics that they fear might trigger controversy and emphasizing expressions that they think might please. Yet they use their writing to share meaning with others, and they enjoy a sense of self-worth and connection as a result. This essay explores the ways that women incarcerated at one state prison use writing to engage with their experience of imprisonment. The voices of the women represented here come from essays they have written as class assignments and articles they have written for the prison newspaper.

MOTIVATIONS FOR PRISON WRITING

Prison writing represents the relationship between the prisoner and the prison, Bob Gaucher argues, noting that writing and other forms of artistic expression "become resistance, a means of survival and a testament to surviving the dislocations of prison life" (2002, 12). Focusing specifically on the prose of imprisoned women, Judith A. Scheffler would agree. She observes, "In an environment where women are too often treated like children, the incarcerated woman writer can maintain some control over her world by ordering reality according to her own perceptions and organizing principles" (2002, xxxv).

Scheffler has developed a schema for classifying women's prison writings. In *Wall Tappings, An International Anthology of Women's Prison Writings 200* [sic] *to the Present*, Scheffler identifies women's prison writing as a significant literary tradition and offers examples of the writings of numerous imprisoned women from different nations and historical periods. She categorizes the motives that inspire the writing of incarcerated women as: vindication of the self; a need to bear witness to prison conditions and deprivations; the struggle for psychological survival through communication and relationships; a desire to maintain family ties and sustain motherhood in prison; a move to solidarity with other women; and transcendence of the prison experience through causes beyond the self (2002, xxi–xliv).

In exploring "vindication of the self" as an impetus, Scheffler notes that prison authors may write "to confirm their own sense of worth, which is essential for any woman writer, but especially empowering for the female outcast, relegated to one of society's most degraded institutions" (2002, xxxiii). Whether or not the writers envision any outside readers for their work, they still believe their thoughts and feelings are worth expressing. In an environment where prisoners' mistakes and poor choices are brought home to them daily and affirmation is practically nonexistent, this is no small belief.

This orientation is expressed by the reflections of some of the journalists in our classes. One mused,

> Who am I? What is my voice? What is my message? . . . Inmate needing to be heard. I'm an inmate growing, changing, needing a voice—a voice to be heard and understood.

Another said she experienced an interest in writing as part of an ongoing personal transformation:

> From as far back as I can remember I had been a timid person with a doormat mentality. But after I came to prison and began to write about my childhood experiences, a flicker of light within me became a flame of passion to write. I feel empowered when I write my piece, and I no longer have a doormat mentality. I found my voice through my writings, and I'm no longer afraid to say, "No, stop, you are hurting me!" When I want to mentally escape this environment, or feel lonely, sad or angry, I write. I write because writing is a true friend to me.

The venue for self-expression that writing offers may allow a female inmate to experience an imagined internal self untouched by the monotonous and degrading routines of prison life.

Incarcerated women are certainly stimulated to testify about the harsh conditions and deprivations they experience in prison. Yet in the context of a prison newspaper, where all articles are read and may be censored by prison administrators prior to publication, this impulse is sometimes tempered by pragmatic self-interest. Why get marked as a troublemaker or a malcontent? Why write articles that will only be cut from the publication? Thus, some women talk about the harsh realities of prison life in journalism class, but don't set them down on paper.

However, the urge to protest is strong, and at times, other women have written about a broad spectrum of prison circumstances. Some have commented on the strip searches, shackles, and solitary confinement imposed on prisoners, while others have written persistently about medical treatment that is difficult to get and the indifferent or incompetent practitioners who deliver it. Other women have focused on the inferior nutrition of the starchy prison diet and the unclean conditions under which it is cooked:

> As to the manner [in] which our food is prepared, the women who work in the kitchen come back and tell us, if we knew how it was prepared, we surely wouldn't eat it. Chicken is a well-liked meal, but if you have to clean it after it is cooked and on your plate, it is just despicable.

Some writers have critiqued the use of heavy doses of medication on inmates with mental health problems, or complained about the lack of education that would prepare prisoners for a better life upon their release. Other writers have complained about insufficient bathroom facilities, the high cost of telephone calls, inconsistent punishments for rule infractions, and many other topics.

Many female inmates write to overcome the social isolation of prison. Writing offers contact with a wider audience, meeting the visceral need for communication and supporting psychological survival. In the prison journalism classes, this phenomenon can be observed in several forms. One author described how writing allowed her to remain a social being after brain damage from a serious accident led to erratic and eventually criminal behavior:

> The only productive outlet I had was to write. So I wrote to save my lonely life, and soul. . . . My behavior is not something that I can easily harness. It is always such a relief when I can write someone and know that, not only will they find me intelligent, but they won't be confused about the person I am on the inside by my sometimes irrational reactions. Why do I write? I write so someone in this world will know who the hell I am.

Another writer explained that her prose enables her to maintain a "sense of normalcy" by connecting her to people and events taking place outside the penitentiary:

It's hard not to develop a "prison mentality" where a person's whole focus is based on what goes on inside these walls. People tend to forget there is an outside world. I want to remind [other inmates] and myself that it is out there and waiting for us.

Some 75 percent of women in prison are mothers, and about two-thirds have children under the age of eighteen (Richie 2002, 139). They have lived through a sudden, forced separation from their families and their longing for their children is often acute. Thus, it is no surprise that the preservation of family relationships should be a motivating factor for imprisoned women. Many of the women involved in the newspaper project have written poems or articles about their families; several have authored ongoing columns that recommend writing as a way of maintaining family ties while incarcerated. In one such column, a writer advises,

You may have no way of knowing whether or not your child is receiving your correspondence, but if there is any chance that your child is receiving your letters, you must continue to write on a regular basis, even if they never respond. . . . That is the biggest purpose of your regular correspondence with your child—to show them your consistent love through your actions.

Others write to pay homage to loved ones on holidays or to remember family members whose love and generosity have touched them.

Regardless of how they lived their lives before prison, once behind bars, many women feel a sense of solidarity with other incarcerated women. This may grow serendipitously among women who have shared a particularly wrenching experience, such as domestic abuse, or it may extend to any incarcerated woman. A special sense of unity seems to evolve out of prison writing workshops, where writing done and shared in community evokes a spirit of resistance and solidarity (Scheffler 2002). One participant in the journalism classes described this joining together in common cause with other inmates. She wrote that the group's efforts to publish a newspaper brought women together with

a lot of encouragement and support for each other. Everybody is from different backgrounds, cultures, their perspectives differ, their religious beliefs are different. And we all come together for one purposes—to produce this newspaper. And to me that is a sense of community.

Another woman wrote, passionately,

> I have learned the urgency of spreading what needs to be said. Our silences will hurt us. Audre Lord, a poet, woman, and a voice that I have become acquainted with while being incarcerated, vowed to be the voice of women who were afraid to speak. My pen has become my voice—the voice that so desperately needs to be heard. . . . Not only for my feelings, my needs; but for all voices.

Together, these prison writers attempt to draw closer to one another while claiming distance from "an institution that labels them worthless and attempts to destroy their humanity in the name of justice," Scheffler remarks (2002, xvii).

OUTCOMES OF PRISON WRITING

When considering the value of writing in other contexts, people often make assumptions about the transformative powers of authorship. Does writing lead to change in the lives of the incarcerated women who do it? To Ann Folwell Stanford, who worked with women in Chicago's Cook County Jail, prison writing is "an act of resistance," an "exercise of power in a place that attempts to deny power to those who are imprisoned there" (2004, 278). But our teaching of journalism at a women's prison leads us to more nuanced observations. As outsiders to the prison world, we can only speculate about why some women join and continue to participate in the writing experience while incarcerated, but there are some outcomes for participants that we can infer. Chief among these are ego gratification, individual attention, and a sense of connection.

We would agree with Scheffler that prison writing brings validation and individual attention to the writer herself. In correctional institutions, personal attention and affirmation are rare; the system recognizes no personal talents or traits. Many incarcerated women have similar experiences of poverty and violence as antecedents to their crimes. A large number of them are survivors of abuse and domestic violence, and their senses of self have been damaged and belittled through victimization. For many participants in the journalism classes, the need to be heard and validated is acute. Lonely women cling to outsiders who visit the prison, who share thoughts and ideas, who bring tangible goods like office supplies, and who express interest in their progress and aspirations. Our sympathies have been appealed to: A woman may say earnestly, "You're the only one who understands what I'm saying," or "If *you* don't help me, no one will." The relational bid is one of needing to be seen and remembered as a unique individual.

Writing may allow a writer to build up her ego, validate her sense of self, and experience a sense of connection to others. Many writers say they feel elated the first time an article bearing their byline appears in the inmate newspaper. By writing for an audience, an author shares parts of her experiences (real or less so, as noted below) with others in her world. She imagines her voice being heard and welcomed by her readers. In the case of a prolific writer with a dedicated audience, the writer and her readers may feel that a relationship exists between them. The population of the prison is small enough that reader feedback from the newspaper makes its way to the writers, often directly. The women in the newspaper group know that their articles will be read not only by the other inmates, but also by corrections officers, teachers, and administrators at the prison, including the superintendent. Copies of the paper are shown to visitors and sometimes mailed to state officials.

In addition, the names of women who regularly attend the class meetings are listed in each issue of the paper, thus giving them distinction even when they have not submitted articles in a given issue of the newspaper. In a sea of nameless, numbered inmates, all dressed the same, all sharing the same dismal living conditions, this special status earns a woman a sense of self. By affiliating herself with a legitimate information-dissemination group, she can be respected as a writer and appreciated by others as an information provider, an expert—an authority.

This "writer" status is often more important than what a woman has written or even if she is *able* to write. While a few women come into prison with excellent formal writing skills, others view writing as an unconquered territory. According to the U.S. Department of Justice, approximately 70 percent of prison inmates perform at the two lowest measurable literacy levels; 11 percent of this group has learning disabilities (2001). Education programs in prisons, especially in women's prisons, are quite limited, often focusing on high school equivalency certification and vocational training. Thus, it is rare for inmate students to develop writing fluencies during incarceration.

Our journalism classes have attracted some women who say they have a desire to write but who seem unable to do it. Several women have taken part in the classes over long periods of time but have never produced any writing. These women seem to enjoy the social *support* for writing, the measure of status offered by the newspaper project, and the small gifts of notepads, pens, and folders they receive in the classes. But they are not actually writing, and we suspect that low literacy skills are the cause.

Most of the women who *are* writing for the inmate newspaper do not show improvement in their writing skills, even after several years of participation. In fact, many are radically opposed to suggestions that a piece of their writing should be edited or revised in any way. When a new issue of the prison newspaper is distributed, participants carefully scrutinize the final product, critically looking for any changes to their work, which they see as insulting. Even if recommendations for revisions come from one of us—college professors who supposedly have superior language skills—the suggestions are generally resisted.

In classes, when the women are asked to comment on each other's writing, most will do no more than offer praise for another writer's piece. If prompted, they say that only the original author knows what she meant and, therefore, no one else has the ability to suggest improvements to her work. These writers fiercely protect the written pieces as extensions of themselves. To be asked to edit or revise is to be criticized at a fundamental level of self-image.

Throughout its history in the United States, inmate writing has attracted the attention of outside readers periodically and has served an important role in improving prison conditions (Morris 2001). But in this project, the prison environment in which we work and the social dynamics it contains have led us to question whether incarcerated writers can create any form of change that takes place outside the mind of the author.

In the prison, writing can be a frustrating exercise. Crowded living spaces afford no quiet or privacy in which to write. Most of the women can't afford or obtain computers, typewriters or, sometimes, even pens and notepads. And no matter what works of art or literary expression prisoners may create, there is no guarantee of continuing ownership of their own work; prison cells are searched often for contraband and any possessions or materials deemed such can be confiscated at any time. Though, as Scheffler theorizes, motivation to write is high in prisons, a variety of factors may mitigate the role of writing as an agent of external change in the authors' lives. Among these, we observe, are unrealistic expectations and the unique workings of self-disclosure in prisons.

Although some of the women harbor fantasies of power, money, or fame derived from writing, there is little evidence of writing as a potent force in the daily life of the prison. A few have sent work to the PEN Prison Writing Contest, while others have read some of the thousands of contemporary books about prison life marketed to popular audiences. For these women, writing may by enjoyable, but there is always the dream that it will lead to a publication, a prize, or a sale. Though several of the women in our classes have had work printed in other prison publications or have been interviewed for books or documentaries made by others, none has earned external fame or fortune through her writing.

Women who hope to use their writing to bring about more immediate and pragmatic empowerment are also often frustrated. Uninformed or unwilling to acknowledge the sheer volume of criminal cases in the courts, some women devote endless hours to the crafting of legal appeals or clemency petitions that rarely bear fruit. Complaints and pleas to legislators or the Commissioner of Corrections are answered with form letters from staffers, a fact not surprising to the politically astute but distressing to desperate inmates. Negative news articles written about living conditions at the prison are often expurgated from the prison newspaper. Thus, it is a struggle for incarcerated women to feel that their writing has consequence.

In our journalism classes, we encourage students to write truthfully, but we do not assume that their writings are factually accurate. People who are not in prison connect to others through the use of self-disclosure, a process that involves reciprocal information sharing about the self with others. However, due to the guarded context in which inmates live, normal ways of sharing information about the self may not be the best way to establish relationships of trust in a correctional institution. Inmates often have no control over the fact that other members of the prison community know many intimate details about their lives.

Thus, in their writings as well as their conversations, inmates may present information that is not true. Safety concerns, a need for privacy, or pursuit of an appearance of power may lead women to practice overt deception or covert manipulation with how they share information about themselves. A writer may craft filtered or even disingenuous narratives, claiming experiences that never happened or re-creating her identity as the person she would prefer to be.

Some of the narratives of women's lives written in the prison may contain sagas of victimization, stories of struggle and redemption, or rationalizations of events and causes and motives that may have little connection to a writer's actual experience. Using resources from the journalism class and a forum established by others, a writer with a manipulative agenda can craft untruths and share them with many readers. Although it is not possible to confirm the accuracy of information published in the prison newspaper, some audience members may assume that these writings are credible because of the setting in which they are disseminated.

It is interesting, given that deception is part of life in a prison, that the perceived and actual consequences of rewriting history are less severe than they would be in other types of writing. An author's relationship with her audience is based on many things—attention, the shared experience of being a prisoner, wanting to reach out to others— yet honesty is not necessarily one of the ingredients. In the forum of shared prison writing, such as that created by an inmate newspaper, a story must ring true to be appreciated, but it need not *be* true.

CONCLUSIONS

In the closed system of the women's prison, all communication is contested and constrained. To the isolated, victimized women who dwell in this world apart, writing is a valuable tool that can be used to create or preserve identity and strengthen a bruised sense of self. Under some circumstances, it attracts praise and recognition. It also can connect one person with others through the sharing of meaning. Thus, many women behind these bars say that writing enables them to make important personal changes. Over time we have witnessed the powerful ongoing appreciation that some women have for the opportunity to write and to share that writing with an audience.

Yet it is also evident that, in this context, the writing of these inmates cannot create the sweeping social change necessary to address their acute socioeconomic, psychological, and physical needs. Historically, inmate writing has served an important role in improving prison conditions, but these reforms have been highly context-specific. They have depended on the convergence of progressive legislators, compassionate superintendents, and committed activists who have come together at opportune moments in history to carry change forward.

Inmate authors need such convergence. They can use writing to strengthen their own egos, experience solidarity with other incarcerated people, and maintain family ties. They can bear witness to the deprivations of prison existence. But until public policy recognizes the human value of prisoners and addresses the educational disadvantage, drug and alcohol addiction, family violence, and mental illness that contribute to crime, their enforced silence will continue.

REFERENCES

Foucault, M. (1979). *Discipline and Punish: The Birth of the Prison*, trans. A. Sheridan. New York: Vintage.

Frey, L. R., Pearce, W. B., Pollock, M., Artz, L., and Murphy, B. A. O. (1996). "Looking for Justice in All the Wrong Places: On a Communication Approach to Social Justice," *Communication Studies* 47: 110–27.

Gaucher, B. (1999). "Inside Looking Out: Writers in Prison," *Journal of Prisoners on Prisons* 10, nos. 1–2: 14–31.

Girshick, L. B. (1999). *No Safe Haven: Stories of Women in Prison.* Boston: Northeastern University Press.

Glaze, L., and Palla, S. (July 2004). *Probation and Parole in the United States, 2003.* U.S. Department of Justice, Bureau of Justice Statistics Bulletin. Retrieved September 10, 2004, online at http://www.csdp.org/research/ppus03.pdf

Harrison, P., and Karberg, J. (May 2004). *Prison and Jail Inmates at Midyear 2003.* U.S. Department of Justice, Bureau of Justice Statistics Bulletin. Retrieved September 10, 2004, online at http://www.ojp.usdoj.gov/bjs/pub/pdf/pjim03.pdf

Human Rights Watch (2003). *Ill-Equipped: U.S. Prisons and Offenders with Mental Illness.* Retrieved September 10, 2004, online at http://www.hrw.org/reports/2003/usa1003/index.htm

Morris, J. M. (2001). *Jailhouse Journalism: The Fourth Estate behind Bars.* New Brunswick, NJ: Transaction.

Pollock, J. M. (2002). *Women, Prison, and Crime*, 2nd ed. Belmont, CA: Wadsworth Thomson Learning.

Richie, B. (2002). "The Social Impact of Mass Incarceration on Women," in *Invisible Punishment: The Collateral Consequences of Mass Imprisonment*, eds. M. Mauer and M. Chesney-Lind. New York: New Press, 136–149.

Scheffler, J. A. (2002). "Introduction," in *Wall Tappings: An International Anthology of Women's Prison Writings 200* [sic] *to the Present*, ed. J. A. Scheffler. New York: Feminist Press at the City University of New York, xxi–xliv.

Sentencing Project, The (2001). *Prisoners Re-entering the Community.* Retrieved June 6, 2002, online at http://www.thesentencingproject.org

Stanford, A. F. (2004). "More Than Just Words: Women's Poetry and Resistance at Cook County Jail," *Feminist Studies* 30, no. 2: 277–301.

Steiner, L. (1992). "The History and Structure of Women's Alternative Media," in *Women Making Meaning: New Feminist Directions in Communication*, ed. Lana Rakow. New York: Routledge, 121–143.

11

TO KEEP MY BODY CLEAN, TO BREATHE, TO GIVE MY MIND REST

Sasha Kamini Parmasad

Emerging out of darkness I arrive at the image of a wooden house against a scarlet sky on the plains of Caroni on the island of Trinidad. This was my home. In the rainy season the floods came; the Caroni River overpowered its banks, ran like a river beneath our house and made the earth swell with water. In the dry season sugarcane was burned and reaped, black cane ashes blew into our house through open windows and doors, the grass turned an orange-brown, and bushfires blazed fiercely on the range of mountains in the north and across the dry Caroni plains. Growing up under that brutal sky in that wooden house, I was sure that I knew every change that came with the seasons; that I could feel the land—nourished by the sweat and tears of my ancestors—breathing beneath my feet when I walked. This was my childhood.

Gone now is that wooden house. Gone are the floods where it once stood. Sugarcane is no longer harvested in the hot months on such a large scale. Everything returns to dust. Almost everything. Because, despite battering time, some impressions persist—of house and sky and rolling cane fields—in the corners of my eyes, in the creases of my flesh. Like a fish I am hooked.

Emerging out of inarticulate depths I discover my voice in this place that ceases to exist with each breath as it passes with its brutal sky, its vibrant drum-beating, jandhi-planting, stick-fighting, storytelling, tan-singing, from one incarnation to the next unseen through the echoing corridors of history. To catch this place, stitch its soul to paper—perhaps this is why I write.

Let me speak as someone still in the process of mastering my craft, figuring out my relation to it. I am a young writer, an amateur: searching, hungry. When I was very young my father, who grew up on one of the last surviving coconut plantations in Trinidad, instilled in me a sense of history. To understand where I stand now I must go back, past childhood, to one moment in the middle of the nineteenth century that is for me the beginning of time. That was the moment when my ancestors—venturing out of famine-stricken villages in the Bhojpuri region of an India, which was ravaged by British colonialism, in search of work and food—were tricked into putting their thumb prints on contracts that designated them indentured laborers, and placed aboard a ship bound for Trinidad. This ship, they were told, would take them to another part of India with ample work where they would be able to save money to bring back to their starving families. It must not have taken them long to discover the treachery of the colonial officials, but the ship could not, would not, be turned back. And so, for three months they fought off the cholera, dysentery, and typhoid that condemned many of their comrades to watery graves while their ship was tossed like a bit of bark across the *kala pani*, the black water, as they called the two tempestuous oceans they crossed. When they set foot in Trinidad they found, instead of a land of sugar, a land of forests and swamps that their white "masters" expected them to tear down, fill up, and make cultivable, profitable. Here they toiled the remainder of their lives on plantations, as did their children and grandchildren (my paternal grandfather). Between 1845 and 1917 approximately 147,000 Indians were brought to Trinidad in degrading, painful conditions of bondage. This experience transformed their deepest conception of themselves and reshaped their intimate relationship with the world. In the process, through their labor and cultural practices, they also transfigured the new landscape to which they had been brought and made it their home. Thus, five generations later, in the evening hours of the twentieth century, I came to be.

But what kind of *being*, this? Very little of the history of Indians in Trinidad was taught at the prestigious primary and secondary schools I attended as a child and young woman through the 1980s and 1990s. What I read in textbooks—that my ancestors had come to Trinidad seeking greener pastures and had been favored with grants of land at the end of their indenture—represented the Indian community as constituting a rich and privileged class. This contradicted the history of our community that was conveyed orally through the stories and songs of hardship and oppression passed down by elders generation after generation. It also contradicted what I experienced living in one of the numerous depressed communities of Indian sugarcane workers and farmers in Trinidad. The textbooks I read distorted the life I knew, sought to silence it. They sought to silence *me*. I should not have been surprised. I should have expected it. Even before birth, after all, I had resisted such attempts.

As my parents told me in my tenth year, the odds were stacked against my being. After graduating from the University of the West Indies in the 1970s my mother and father went to live and engage in political work in the heart of the plantation belt of Trinidad among sugarcane workers and farmers. Like many university graduates in those days they earned their livelihood as teachers. When my mother became pregnant with me she was a teacher at a Roman Catholic secondary school in Central Trinidad. As an activist, she sought to raise the level of consciousness of the students about issues affecting them and the wider society. For this the school authorities sought to punish her in the most inhumane way. The school principal tried to conceal from my mother the fact that there was an outbreak of German measles in the school. Caring nothing for the unborn child in my mother's womb, these goodly, godly Roman Catholics tried to deny me my place in the world; for, as my mother told me, had she been infected her doctor had advised her that she would have had to make some hard decisions. And so, although all the tests proved negative, my mother still awaited my birth with apprehension until she finally held me—with ten perfect toes and fingers as she put it—in her arms.

As a result of their political activism my parents lost their government teaching jobs and almost lost me. Growing up beneath a brutal sky on the plains of Caroni it sometimes seemed as if I was always fighting, struggling against attempts to silence my voice. In the face of such attacks, words became my only defense.

* * *

Before I began to write, I began to recite. At the age of six, I began reciting folk poems written by my father on national television and from the age of eight I was singing calypsos written by him at public competitions and cultural programs in different parts of Trinidad. Taking my father's words into my mouth, performing them, I rearticulated them, possessed them, invested them with new meaning. They also possessed me. An exchange took place in which the rhythms and cadences of his words became my own. Memorizing his words, learning to dramatize them, I arrived at such an intimacy with them that I often felt they had come from me. Only through this appropriation was I able to perform to the best of my ability, with heart and soul involved. This is significant because of what my father wrote—poems, calypsos, and Indian folk songs that spoke out against racism, discrimination, the oppression of the poor, apartheid, and American cultural imperialism; these chronicled the suffering of the oppressed, which included the Indian community in Trinidad and the rich heritage that they fought to retain. My parents believed in exposing me to—not shielding me from—the events of the world. In singing my father's songs I learned about the brutalities of colonialism and the struggles waged by my indentured ancestors; about P. W. Botha committing murder in South Africa; about the children of Soweto; about the landing of American troops in Grenada; and about the racism experienced by Indians in Guyana. Despite their storminess and internal darkness, my father's songs and poems always ended with a message of hope pointing to the responsibility of each new generation to continue the struggle to rectify inequalities in Trinidadian society. His themes—oppression, discrimination, persistent struggle, endurance—became my themes when I began to write at the age of eight or nine. I copied his words, his metaphors and similes, as young artists, apprenticed to professional painters, mimic the style of their teachers. Perhaps it was natural that I took to these themes so quickly, because the things that I sang about were not so removed from what I myself experienced and saw around me, growing up in that small wooden house in a rural village in the heart of a poor, depressed community.

From very early on my parents decided to expose me to as many of the cultural forms of Trinidad and Tobago—especially African and Indian forms—as they had been exposed to themselves. I began learning kathak, an Indian classical dance form, at the age of six and was soon singing Indian folk songs composed by my father. I entered the calypso arena as a little girl in 1986, singing and placing first at a cultural festival held under the banner of the Association of Progressive Youth, a cultural organization working among young people in Trinidad. It was not strange for my father to write calypsos or for my mother to train me to sing them. They had both grown up appreciating calypso and steelband music in their hometowns, and before I was born my father had given his calypsos to older, experienced performers to sing. In 1987 I entered the competitive National Junior Queen Calypso competition, held under the auspices of the National Women's Action Committee, and placed second in the final round. I was the first Indian child to enter any such arena in Trinidad and my participation evoked both positive and negative responses from the predominantly African Trinidadian adult audiences before whom I performed.

Indians constitute the single largest community in Trinidad (by two or three percent), yet Indian cultural practices receive only token inclusion in the "national culture" of my country. And ironically, though the calypso is promoted as the national song form, it is largely those Indian performers who negate themselves that are tolerated in the calypso arena. Additionally, Indians often have to face racist, anti-Indian calypsos during the annual Carnival season. This overt hostility has led some Indian performers to seek alternative spaces for themselves. Though the situation was not this blatant fifteen years ago when I was performing and though there were many in the audience that appreciated and welcomed my singing, others saw it as an unwanted incursion into their domain and were quick to call me "coolie" (a derogatory term equivalent to "nigger") and shout at me to get off the stage. Controversies of one kind or another cropped up around me each year that I sang. For certain programs my name was repeatedly the only one excluded from the list of performers printed in the newspapers and in cases when it was mentioned it was invariably misspelled.

But these negative experiences did not lessen my love for the artform or the satisfaction I derived from singing about issues that I thought really mattered. Instead, at the age of nine, they filled me with a desire to sing sweeter and louder and longer, and to throw my voice into every corner of the country. In public I sang and in private I wrote poems to fortify myself, to ward off hopelessness and private frustration, to voice—assert, articulate—myself to myself. Writing was my shield, magical and secret. It gave me a feeling of power and allowed me to see and make myself through my own eyes. I thought that I could write myself out of anything, and into being as brave or as strong as I wanted to be. I remember once getting up in the middle of the night unable to sleep, my body damp with sweat. I was so agitated that I had to sit and write in what I called my "poem book." I was ten. I still have a copy of the poem, titled the "The Monster of the Storm." At the end of it I inscribed this little note to myself: "This poem refers to the racial government of Trinbago and the Indians trying to keep up their culture; the monster and storm [are] the government and the person struggling [represents] . . . the Indian [community]."

In Trinidad, Indians are often referred to as "East Indians." Growing up, I was bewildered and pained by this definition of myself: an East Indian Trinidadian from the West Indies. Though the indigenous peoples of Trinidad had been decimated by the Spanish conquistadors, and all others who came to consider the island their home were people transplanted from other places, relations of power in the society had caused African Trinidadians to be cast as "native" and Indians as "alien." In the face of this form of representation, using writing to present myself to myself was not enough. I wanted to use it to engage the wider society—the dominant, hegemonizing "other"—on my own terms. I felt the need to contest the received knowledge of myself and the accompanying images and representations that were shaped by essentialized colonial Eurocentric/North American values. In the eyes of mainstream Trinidad, these were notions that the community that I came from was docile, backward, alien, and "uncultured" in its practices. Though I was filled with these amorphous yearnings, nothing came of them for many years. I continued to write poems to myself and wait for the future, occasionally asking my parents to critique my efforts.

Though the Indian cultural formation in Trinidad developed out of an oral folk tradition, there was widespread reverence for the sacred texts—the Ramayana, the Mahabharata, the Qu'ran—that some had managed to bring with them from India. Although most Indians at that time were not literate in English, many could invariably recite entire passages from the Ramayana and other sacred texts by heart. Indentured laborers literate in Hindi, Urdu, or English had been respected and had usually been appointed leaders of, and spokespersons for, the masses. The capacity to read and write gave them a greater consciousness of their rights and some power over their destinies—for example, the ability to petition the governor about issues or write letters to the local newspapers.[1] In the first quarter of the 1900s some Indians "'risk[ed] their children's conversion' [to Christianity] for the chance of an education" and "it was through representation by those who had used the Presbyterian opportunity for education, that [the community] continued to clamour for schools and institutions, including a press that identified with their needs."[2] Certainly, they were seeking to access the dominant language of colonialism, the better to contest their condition of colonial subordination.

I became more personally aware of the acute power wielded by words in another way. You see, I slept on a wide hollow bed that my father had built to store stacks of illicit communist books. On occasion the mattress would be raised and the wooden planks removed, and I would climb into the bed with my father to search for this or that. Some of the books were mildewed and torn; silverfish slithered through the spines of others, but each book was precious. People had taken great risks, gone to great pains to access and procure many of them; it was also true that one could be arrested and imprisoned for owning them. Books could do this—send you to prison. At six years of age, at eight and ten, what greater evidence did I need of the power of words?

Though my parents never told me, I instinctively knew that certain words I had grown up hearing, that often peppered conversations in our intimate circle of friends, could be mentioned to no one outside the domain of our house. Terms like *revolution, communist, imperialist, socialist, class struggle,* and *Marxism* were dangerous, could get people into trouble with the police. I watched and censored the words I uttered to teachers and children at school, to neighbors, even as I tried through my writing to break through the layers of silence always threatening to enclose me. Stories, involving specific characters and incidents, I could not manage—I found the writing too direct, too readable. I turned to poetry, hunted down metaphors and similes, and watched my words.

That was one thing. I also became aware of the power of words through my father. When my father gave speeches at community gatherings or cultural programs—reminding people to fight for equality, to take pride in their heritage, the practices preserved with such love by their ancestors despite repression—his passionate words always drove some to tears. I remember old women in the audience with *orhinis* (veils) draped over their heads, and old men in khaki pants, approaching my father after a speech and taking his hand or patting his back, tears rolling down their cheeks. It filled me with awe that words could have that effect on people, could uplift and strengthen them, fill them with resolve. My father continued making speeches, but at some point during my teenage years I came to realize that his words, though so powerful, melted in the air. I realized that generations would follow that would not find in any book the histories or stories he recounted and interpreted. Though his spoken words reached masses of laboring people in a way that his written words would not ever have, his speeches left too much up to memory at a time when oral traditions were beginning to be eroded. In my childhood, storytelling was still used by elders in the Indian community as a primary means of preserving history and transmitting knowledge from one generation to the next. However, there was also the consciousness that such cultural practices were beginning to wear away as televisions entered homes and patterns of life changed. Perhaps it was an anxiety about such cultural loss that steered me toward the written form over the oral, such as reciting. It was obvious to me that words were powerful things and equally obvious (in light of my father's experience) that it would be better to try to preserve them on paper rather than let them dissipate in the air. A voice committed to paper, multiplied in even a thousand copies of a book, is more difficult to silence than a man speaking spontaneously on a podium. From early on, the notion developed in me that writing offered a greater chance of continuity than orality allowed. This notion cemented my will to record what I could of my existence in the world.

I grew up surrounded by fragments—rhymes and riddles, family histories, foods, folktales, games, music, songs, rituals, cultural practices—that our ancestors had brought with them from India and passed on to later generations. Writing about the historical formation of Caribbean civilization, the writer Derek Walcott notes, "Break a vase, and the love that reassembles the fragments is stronger than that love which took its symmetry for granted when it was whole."[3] It was with a profound and enduring love that succeeding generations of Indians in Trinidad reassembled, reconstituted the cultural fragments that they had preserved and guarded with such care, shaping them into a new whole. Perhaps, among other things, it is a similar desire or instinct to reconstitute—to patch up time, knit a scarlet sky, a wooden house, fragments of personal and inherited memory into a cohesive, more stable, continuous whole—that drove me to write as a child and continues to drive me today.

Feeling preceded language, for my father and for me, though I acquired the tools of written language much earlier than he did. He grew up in the barracks of St. Joseph Estate, one of the last operating coconut plantations in Trinidad, and learned to read at a relatively late age. He became the first person in his family to study beyond third or fourth grade and devoured books with a hunger. By the time he acquired the tools he needed to write, my father had many lifetimes of things to document and to say—on his own behalf and that of his parents and grandparents. He decided to become a historian. Much of the history of the Indians in Trinidad was unrecorded, and as elders died they took whole worlds with them. A feeling of urgency propelled all his reading and writing. In this context I am reminded of what Nadine Gordimer has written about black writers in South Africa: "All the obstacles and diffidences—lack of education, a tradition of literary expression, even the chance to form the everyday habit of reading that germinates a writer's gift— [were] overcome by the imperative to give expression to a majority not silent, but one whose deeds and whose proud and angry volubility against suffering [had] not been given the eloquence of the written word."[4] This, I think, is one of the feelings that drew my father inexorably to writing. Eventually, he published some of his poems, and the first collection of Indian folktales of the Caribbean, but the more pressing demands of his political activism—and later, of work, of picking up the pieces, earning a living—did not allow him to write or record as much as he wanted, as much as was needed. Seeing this I told myself, Now it's up to you, girl. Of course I had been writing madly, filling large notebooks from cover to cover for years—just for myself, just to be able to breathe easily, to fight against invisibility, to release the secrets stored up inside me, to break through the silence, to see myself through my own eyes, ward off loneliness—so this decision to shoulder the responsibility of "voicing," of giving a written presence to my world and the life experiences of Indians in my community, was not really a sudden decision. I had been doing just this all along—writing from my gut, my liver, in loud thunderbolts and flashes of lightning.

In 1988, I moved with my family to New Delhi, India, and lived there for four years between the ages of ten and fourteen. I continued to perform there—to sing, dance, and recite—but my activities were limited mostly to my school and the university campus where we lived. The intense performing life I had led in Trinidad suddenly slowed down and, as if to fill the gap, I began to write with intensity. Perhaps this drive was a symptom of the same old thing—the desire to "voice," to be seen and understood on my own terms. The first year was difficult, and I encountered numerous misconceptions at the English-medium school that I attended. When I told children in my class that I was from the West Indies (understandably they did not know where Trinidad, a mere inkblot on their atlas, was) they often looked confused and sometimes disbelieved me outright. When I asked them why, they told me that I had the wrong kind of hair (my hair was too straight) and that I looked Indian, not "West Indian" like people on the West Indies cricket team. When I said that I *was* West Indian, one particular boy said, "Oh! You mean you are from West India!" Others refused to believe that Indians constituted the largest single population group in Trinidad. When I pointed out that Alvin Kallicharran, who had been on the West Indies cricket team a few years earlier, was Indian like me, those who checked with their parents agreed and had nothing else to say. It disturbed me that they were not too interested in knowing what "my kind of Indian" was. Even when (following the advice of my parents) I explained how Indians had come to be in Trinidad, some still referred to me as an NRI (a non-resident Indian—my classmates either admired NRIs or disdained them) and were offended that I did not know any Indian language.

I continued to poke the fire. Aware that most of the students belonged to the higher castes, I told them I was a low-caste *sudra* because my foreparents had been sudras, but most dismissed what I said because I was from the West and therefore did not seem to carry the stigma of an Indian-born sudra. We were children, self-righteous and stubborn. My parents explained that I had to be patient, but I flew into many fits of rage at school that first year and got into several fights that I can laugh about now only with a moderate degree of humor. It was shocking for me to discover how invisible the Indian Trinidadian community and its struggles were to the rest of the world—even to those in my ancestral homeland. I could never comprehend how the whole history of Indian indenture was absent from the consciousness of those Indians we encountered in India at that time. Removed from Trinidad, much of my creative writing became centered on that place. I began to write with a greater awareness of addressing an audience that was "other." I wrote to give myself audibility and presence in the world.

Later, when I returned to Trinidad and began studying history at the secondary school level I was appalled by the absences that I found. I learned everything about slavery, I learned about the Haitian revolution, about the kingdoms of West Africa, the maroons in Jamaica, the intricacies of the French Revolution but hardly anything—just a smattering—about the history and struggle of my ancestors in Trinidad. I do not think that it was the teachers' fault; it was the nature of the syllabus we were taught. We learned about the significance of African emancipation, little about Indian indenture. We were exposed to the developmental history of Carnival but not told the ways in which the indentured laborers and their descendants had reconstituted and reshaped their own festivals—Diwali, Phagwa, Ramleela, Hosay—in the new landscape of Trinidad. The education system provided me with little opportunity for self-knowledge but rather promoted self-negation. In this situation, Indian-Trinidadian students were easily seduced almost by design, one might say, to accept the representations of themselves presented by others. For example, at one of the prestigious Port-of-Spain secondary schools that I attended, neither black nor white students openly used derogatory terms to refer to each other.

However, they used such terms (like "aaloo pie") as a matter of course to refer to Indians. What was more disturbing was that some Indian students who had been admitted into the "popular" white and the black circles often used these deprecating terms to refer to other Indian students. I found it revolting.

It is fortunate that from a very young age, through the influence of my parents and others, I became acutely aware that there was an alternative, positive way of viewing myself and my relationship with the world. Much of the history of my community I learned from my parents, grandparents, and elders in the village in which I grew up. I also accessed this history in a more visceral way through authors such as Ismith Khan, Harold Sonny Ladoo, V. S. Naipaul, and Samuel Selvon. In the school environment, literature was the only space in which I found my community represented, in which I was able to see reflections of myself in books such as Naipaul's *A House for Mr. Biswas* and Khan's *The Jumbie Bird*. I was elated and proud that these books gave me an opportunity to engage my presence in Trinidad in a creative way in the classroom, a space that often offered me only negative representations of myself. I also felt oppressed, burdened by what I knew of the history of my community in Trinidad; I wished to share this knowledge with others, to correct teachers, but had neither the authority nor the forum to do so. This filled me with a kind of blankness. This remarkable exclusion, this invisibility, this feeling of voicelessness filled me with a maddening need to use my writing not as a shield but as a weapon to contest the historical marginalization of a whole people and the negation of my experiences as an Indian in Trinidad. Simply the act of claiming a voice for myself became an act of contestation.

* * *

Coming from the margins, writing is a subversive act that allows me to contest distorted images of myself and my community manufactured by those hegemonizing forces that have historically relegated Indians in Trinidad to oppressive relations of voicelessness and invisibility. Though I am physically removed from my home at the present time, all of my writing is concentrated on this small piece of land, the place that best knows both my pain and my laughter. For many oppressed and marginalized peoples, simply the act of writing, of "voicing"—presenting their experiences to the world through their own eyes—is a revolutionary act. For a people whose experiences have been historically marginalized, just having a voice represents a qualitative change.

In a sense, Indians in Trinidad have always had a voice; each generation has given rise to its own agents who have voiced the pain and suffering of the community. However, language for us has always been a way of presenting ourselves to ourselves, of sustaining our spirits. This speaking to ourselves helped to consolidate community—strengthen cultural practices, build new self-images, develop metaphors and idioms that allowed us to understand and possess our world—but was not directed at engaging the dominant "other" in ways that forced the "other" to pay heed to us. We engaged the notion of the "other" among ourselves but did not often engage the "other" in actuality. In my own family, both my grandfather and my great-grandmother composed Bhojpuri songs about their experiences and performed these within the community. But their words, as powerful and meaningful as they were, were never allowed to make the transition beyond the boundaries of community. Like the Indian Trinidadian people themselves, their words fell victim to marginalization and subordination, and were readily contained on the social and cultural periphery. Some may argue that this marginalization was the natural result of their singing songs in Bhojpuri/Hindi, not English. However, mainstream Trinidad society has always embraced *parang*, songs celebrating the Nativity of Christ that are sung in Spanish, a language understood by very few Trinidadians, even teaching this song form in schools. As was shown in the case of those indentured Indians who "risk[ed] their children's conversion [to Christianity]" to acquire the language of power,[5] there has always been the need to acquire new linguistic tools in order to contest the "other" occupying the dominant mainstream. This enterprise, however, imposes many stringent demands on the young writer struggling for her distinctive, authentic voice, her own mode of representing her world. The real challenge continues to be how to engage this process on one's own terms, avoiding the pitfalls of self-alienation. How to engage it without being ruptured from one's moorings or internalizing the dominant perspectives of the "other."

To conclude, I say, writing is my attempt to engage the world on my own terms, to see myself and my community through my own eyes and present this image to the world. I repeat these words to myself, I mull over them. They ring true. And yet there is something missing. To tear off the shroud of mystery surrounding my desire to write I say, "It is this, it is this and this" that leads me to put words to paper. I make my writing process a figural sculpture and walk around it, examining it from a multiplicity of perspectives. When I stand here, the right arm is very prominent and seems of particular importance, but when I shift to the front I notice the expression in the eyes and think that this must be the key to understanding everything. Slowly, step by step, I circle the sculpture only to realize that it is not any one of these things that is important but perhaps all of them together . . . and something more. Then why do I write? In truth, the process eludes my understanding. I cannot pin it down; my lens feels too narrow. After I have said all this I think it would be most truthful to say that I write to keep my body clean; to be able to breathe, because the air gets fresher when strained of words; to give my mind rest, because having strings of words tramping about the inside of my head keeps me up at night.

12

DIARY OF A MAD LAW STUDENT

Jodi Bromberg

There should be a warning label on law school applications that explains the limits of the law to prospective law students interested in social justice work. The label would say that it is impossible to reform a broken system, so that students know this before entering the profession. We continue to perpetuate the myth of social justice through the law. This myth is necessary in part to entice the many students who enter law school each year to try and "change the world" by being lawyers and who might not otherwise fill up university classrooms and coffers with tuition dollars, and later, alumni contributions. Unfortunately, most of those law students, because of the hegemonic nature of law school and the legal profession, end up perpetuating the system they entered school to try to dismantle.

I wrote this essay because it is a way to make sense of the last three years of law school, and the way that a legal education has changed my thinking and perspective on the potential efficacy for using the law to fight for social justice. I write as a way to make sense of the crazy world I find myself living in today. I write this essay because I need to bear witness to the experience of being a progressive white Jewish lesbian law student in the first years of the twenty-first century. This is my story. This is why I write.

I walked into my first evening of law school wearing surfing shorts, a black t-shirt, a summer tan, and a shaved head. I had just driven seven hours from Provincetown, Massachussetts, the tip of Cape Cod, where I spent the summer after quitting my job of six years as a magazine editor. I looked around my first Legal Decision-Making class: the men were a sea of khaki pants and button-down shirts. The women wore some variety of business casual, typically black pants and a sweater set.

I entered law school purposefully trying to mark myself as "other," as a way to remind myself of the perspective I brought to law school. I didn't want to lose that perspective, and I was aware of the way that the educational methods of law schools are purposefully created to retrain the thinking of students. I had wanted to go to law school since the summer I watched my first murder trial, just after my eleventh birthday. The man who killed my twelve-year-old cousin Katie had been on trial for her murder, after they found her bloody underwear balled up inside his dresser drawer. The jury convicted him of second-degree murder without ever finding a body, one of the only juries in Virginia's history to ever do so.

Watching that trial, I had a little girl's version of justice and the law. The bad man ended up in jail, behind bars, where he couldn't hurt anyone else's playmate. It was rooted in easy notions of good and bad. I kept those ideas for a long time, spurred on by the popular 1980s television drama, *L.A. Law,* and a public school education that emphasized the important role that the law had in social change—mainly through discussions about desegregation, the end of Jim Crow laws, and reproductive freedom. So, like many of my classmates, I went to law school because I wanted to help people, to right injustices, and in a post-civil rights era, *of course* you would do that through the law.

But the law school indoctrination into becoming part of the legal system, even as I might seek to change it, is both subtle and swift. It begins on the first day and continues for three years. All graduate school programs have their own jargon, their own way of telescoping the problems of the world through their lens of specialty. Law school is no different in that respect, and at first, it was disorienting, seemingly purposefully so. It took an hour to read six pages, with *Black's Law Dictionary* at my side. I was nervous in classes when professors called on me.

The predominant pedagogical method in most law schools remains some variation on the Socratic method. But even in classes where the Socratic method is not used, the foci of the classroom lectures or discussions still typically revolves around the casebook method: reading cases and analyzing them for their predictive value so that students learn to make legal arguments by analogizing or distinguishing their case from the existing precedents.

Students in most law schools across the country learn the same subjects during their first year: contracts, torts, constitutional law, civil procedure, criminal law, and, in some form, legal research and writing. These are the building blocks for lawyers. Law is still taught, at least in my second-tier state institution, as if it were a trade: here are the tools, and here is how to use them. Carpenters do not learn to question the value or utility of their hammer during their vocational education, and neither do lawyers learn to question the utility of the underlying structure of the U.S. legal system.

What neither the Socratic nor casebook methods do is provide students with much of an opportunity to contemplate justice as it might be, or to talk about the inevitable alienation and frustration they might feel as they recognize the law's limitations. The law is by its nature conservative and slow to change, but it is by and large not seen as such by students who grew up in the post-civil rights era. The law continues to reinforce institutional and societal discrimination and privilege and often perpetuates inequities among races, classes, and genders. For example, throughout law school, I was acutely aware of the ways my relationship with another woman was disadvantaged and left unprotected by state and federal laws. In this way, the law continues to be used as a tool to encourage and institutionalize some behaviors while disadvantaging and discounting others. Yet there are far too few discussions in most law school classrooms about the impact of this on law students, lawyers, judges, and society in general.

Instead, the casebook method is rooted deeply in the predictive value of the law: we learn what the courts will decide in the future based on what they have decided in the past. Law students are taught to predict outcomes. This creates a system where we begin to see the system before us as being part of the natural order of things. Our expectations become entrenched in the slow pace of change, and we lose the ability to dream the big dreams of a just world or legal system. It is this hegemony of the law school experience that I was not quite prepared for: the way that law students, including myself, become willing to accept what was once unacceptable.

Law school's disorientation—learning new jargon and a new way of thinking—serves to redefine entrants as "law students," so that they "think like lawyers." The resulting reorientation then quickly limits the scope with which students might envision change. It becomes more difficult to think about the law *outside* of a casebook framework, outside of a structure that inherently limits one's thinking about the possibilities for revolutionary change. This experience occurs both within and outside of the classroom, and both within the law school itself and the larger legal community.

For example, while many students may enter law school as I did, intent on doing public-interest work, they often succumb to the social and economic pressures to instead join a large law firm. These firms predominantly represent large corporations and wealthy individuals, though many have a nominal commitment to pro bono work. My law school, like many others, offers a generous scholarship to students who intend to do public-interest work after graduation. Yet a significant number of those students ultimately choose not to pursue public-interest law but instead to repay their loans and enter the far more lucrative world of corporate law. I am no different; though I entered law school focused exclusively on public-interest work, I accepted a position last fall to join the 150-attorney firm I worked at last summer. While I believe that it is the right decision for me, and I am satisfied with that, I think it is useful to examine the environment in which I made that decision. I think this is useful predominantly because of the frequency with which this experience occurs in law schools in the United States.

Currently, students are encouraged to pursue on-campus interviewing (OCI) in the fall of their second year for the upcoming summer. Students are told that this is an important job, as firms make postgraduation job offers to their summer associates. Economic stability after law school then becomes tied to the summer employment students are able to obtain after their second year of law school. Particularly at second-tier schools like mine, there is an undercurrent of worry throughout the student body and administration about students finding gainful employment after graduation, and this often plays heavily into students' decisionmaking process.

OCI requires students to submit their résumés in July after their first year, and students who do well academically in their first year are typically rewarded with several interviews. In fact, the year I participated in OCI, I saw the same familiar faces for interview after interview. Those students who are not at the top of their class at second-tier schools are, frustratingly, largely left out of this process. But anyone may submit their résumés to participate in OCI, and the process is ridiculously easy to do. To throw her hat in the ring for OCI, a student must only upload her résumé, request her transcript, and choose which employers to send it to. However, in addition to the selective nature of the interview process, the employers who attend OCI are almost exclusively large Philadelphia corporate law firms. These firms compensate their summer associates at a range of $1,000 to $2,400 per week, earning $10,000 to $24,000 per summer. Law students offered positions typically must give their potential employer a decision no later than December 1. After participating in OCI, if successful, it becomes difficult for law students who have done well academically to imagine a different outcome than working at a large law firm. After all, the large law firms are *prestigious!* The lawyers are *rich!* The workload is *intellectually stimulating!* It becomes difficult to see why a law student with the opportunity to work at a big law firm would want to do anything else.

On the other hand, few public-interest jobs exist, and those that do typically do not interview candidates until after winter break. Public-interest organizations for the most part do not participate in OCI. Despite the competent and helpful public-interest office at my school, applying for these summer positions requires fortitude on the part of law students: they must figure out which agencies are hiring, who the contact person is, and when the deadlines are, and then write cover letters and send out résumés and transcripts individually, envelope by envelope. It also requires a leap of faith to bypass OCI, or turn down an offer from a firm to pursue the later public-interest job cycle. In a competitive job market, coming from a non-elite institution, the impact of this timing issue on students should not be underestimated.

In addition, if a public-interest position is secured (because they are often *more* competitive than their law firm counterparts) it is typically unfunded or funded with work-study. As a result, students must frequently pursue outside funding options to create economically viable employment. Most students I knew who did this at my school pursued Student Public Interest Network grants (which carry their own workloads, in terms of volunteer hours, in exchange for the grant), and typically earned about $3,500 to $4,000 for the summer. (Remember, this is compared to the $10,000 to $24,000 their classmates would make at a large law firm.)

Relatedly, these public-interest agencies typically do not have entry-level positions, so there is no offer of employment at the end of the summer. Instead, work after graduation largely depends on securing one of the few public-interest fellowships available that pay salaries of one-third to one-quarter of their law firm counterparts. These fellowships are highly competitive, attracting students from elite and non-elite institutions all over the country. They carry with them their own separate arduous application and selection process. When you add to these factors the tremendous educational debt that most students graduate with and again, the general anxiety of finding gainful legal employment when coming from a second-tier law school, it becomes even more difficult to make the decision to pursue work at a public-interest agency.

Furthermore, there is an assumption (based in fact) made by most faculty that most students will end up working for private law firms that represent corporate interests, and as such, their teaching is often skewed toward that perspective. This is a subtle but nonetheless important influence on law students: few hypothetical scenarios start out, "Your client is on public assistance, has $25,000 in credit card debt, and is about to be evicted," or, "Your client has just been fired because she is transgender and is transitioning from male to female."

A related point is the way that the law has historically treated disenfranchised or disempowered people and the impact this has on law students' decisionmaking process about their employment prospects after graduation. For example, in my first-year writing class, our first legal assignments involved a hypothetical scenario about a series of news stories and debates posted in an Internet chat room, and some additional information about one of the men who participated in the debate. The assignment—typical for law school—was to research all of the possible legal issues it raised and write a memo about them. The man I theoretically represented was, among other things, falsely called gay.

I found out that, in many states, falsely calling someone *gay* is defamation per se. That means that on its very face, it is defamation, like calling someone a thief or a drug dealer. The plaintiff in such cases did not have to prove that being called gay was damaging to his reputation; it was assumed that such damage occurred.

Of course, it makes sense: lesbian, gay, bisexual, and transgender (LGBT) people are faced with discrimination every day. There are real consequences to being openly queer: in most states, it is legal to fire, evict, or deny employment to someone simply because they are gay or lesbian. The defamation per se laws just commodify that loss and make it possible for people who are wrongly identified as gay or lesbian to recover monetary damages for that discrimination. The defamation laws make it possible for people who have suffered some harm for being called *gay*—but who aren't—to be awarded money from those who caused the harm. Meanwhile, we "real gays" continue to suffer also from discrimination and harm, but unlike our "fake gay" counterparts, we can't recover for it. Learning about the way that the law has historically treated, and continues to treat, the disenfranchised and disempowered of course shapes our thinking on the outer limits of what we see as possible, because we are, of course, working within that very system. It also plays a part in what students see as possible in their own lives. If students are offered positions at big law firms, and are used to being or feeling like outsiders, disenfranchised from the law, it may be more tempting to want access to the privilege and prestige that large firms offer.

Any student who works at both a "big" law firm and a public-interest agency quickly notices the stark differences between the two. On the one hand, resources are typically cobbled together, and the lawyers on staff must undertake a variety of administrative tasks, which might range from copying and collating to mailing out their own packages, ordering their own office supplies, or fixing their own computer. On the other hand, at big law firms, as one professor told me, "lawyers are paid just to think" in an environment that I can only explain as grossly consumptive: There are whole departments set up to photocopy documents; there are librarians to help guide legal research; there are rooms full of computers that are only used for training; there is a mail room with couriers to take files down the hall, or to the next floor; there are assistants to type correspondence or documents, and information technology specialists to call with computer problems. Certainly, most students, even those inclined to work for social justice, find it difficult to resist the allure of such posh and plentiful resources.

It seems to me that these disparities exist in part because members of the bar have collectively lost any ability to envision a markedly different way. Of course, public-interest jobs are limited! Of course, they are more difficult to obtain! Of course, they face vastly limited resources! This is the way things are; it is the way the legal system has always been.

As a result, public-interest agencies are funded just enough to keep alive the myth of "law as social justice." It is a myth because while we continue to perpetuate the *idea* of social justice and the *goals* of social justice, we do comparatively little as a profession to systematically encourage law students to pursue this route, to pursue justice under the law. Instead, the systems encourage the perpetuation of existing systems of privilege, domination, and subordination. Thus, while social justice is sometimes obtained in individual cases, it continues to remain elusive under the law in any systemic or institutional sense, in part because of the limited vision with which law students (who of course then become lawyers) are taught to see what is possible.

While students might then choose to work for social justice within a public-interest organization, they do so having already been indoctrinated by the hardships and limited resources of such positions. This leads not only to fewer students pursuing this avenue but also to their having a reduced vision of what is possible: the limited resources of public-interest work are normative and accepted, though of course, no one is explicitly pro-poverty or pro-discrimination.

Relatedly, students are taught to perfect the casebook method of analysis, of issue spotting, or predicting how a court might rule in a case based on precedent. This also limits the change in the system that students might envision. First, they are taught that if they are to try and seek change, it must be slowly, one building block following another. *Brown v. Board of Education* and *Roe v. Wade* are taught with all due reverence for their architects, perhaps appropriately so. At the same time, there is a legend surrounding these cases: they are the success stories of a generation of civil rights activists about the availability of social justice under the law.

Here, even the legend of what is heralded as the best of what the law can be limits our thinking in its teaching and reference. In these specific cases, the precedents ring hollow now as, fifty or thirty years later, the holdings in these cases have been severely limited in scope.

By this, I mean to refer to the scholarship of Derrick Bell, Peter Irons, and others that has arisen in a post-*Brown* era underscoring the ongoing segregation of public schools in the United States and the economic disadvantages that schools with predominantly African-American and Latino/a students continue to face. Similarly, there is the *idea* of reproductive freedom for women in the United States, but according to the Alan Guttmacher Institute, 87 percent of U.S. counties have no abortion provider. Additionally, most states do not cover abortions under Medicaid except in cases of incest, rape, or life endangerment, severely limiting the ability of low-income women to have abortions. The result is that the laws of desegregation and reproductive freedom exist but are, practically speaking, rapidly becoming impotent.

Thus, the ideology of a teaching that surrounds the legend of these "success stories" makes it structurally difficult for law students to envision a different plan that might be necessary to pursue justice under the law. Its effect is to limit our thinking to the very small path we are taught to travel in law school through the predictive value and nature of law rather than exploring the underlying value of the legal system as it exists and envisioning either an entirely more just system or, at least, a way toward a new path for social justice.

13

A DRAWBRIDGE TO THE IVORY TOWER: BROKERING THE POLITICS OF ENVIRONMENTAL STUDIES

Daniel J. Sherman

When I was a graduate student, my dog accompanied me as I criss-crossed rural America in a fifteen-year-old Mazda 323 hatchback to conduct fieldwork in communities chosen to host low-level radioactive waste disposal sites. Many of the people I interviewed in these communities displayed extraordinary hospitality by offering me a place to stay and providing meals for both my dog and me. However, before I ever achieved this level of acceptance in these communities, most of my interviewees asked me why I write—though none of them used those exact words.

When Bobby Lee, a retired used car salesman, asked that I provide him with a notarized letter stating that I was not an agent for the Federal Bureau of Investigation, he was, in essence, asking me why I write.[1] Bobby also requested that I provide biographical information and that I disclaim any association with a long list of government agencies and utility companies before he would consent to an interview. His preinterview screening process was not typical in its formality, but it was typical in its scope of inquiry. Bobby and the rest of my interviewees wanted to know two things about my writing: why I was interested in the topic, and what I was going to do with the information I obtained. My access to the communities I studied depended on my answers to these two questions. Now that my research is complete and my dissertation is finished, I am asking myself these critical questions in an effort to find a balance between my academic responsibilities and my responsibilities to the communities I study.

This chapter will consider my answers to these two "why I write" questions—both during and after my research. What follows is not a dispassionate analysis of the ethical dilemmas inherent in human subject research, nor is this a practical primer on fieldwork. Instead, I will provide a personal reflection on the process of both conducting fieldwork in small communities and then determining how best to use the results of that fieldwork. In doing so, I attempt to explore the politics of writing as I trace the way strategic research decisions have shaped my relationships with numerous individuals and communities, and the way these relationships are currently shaping my scholarly production and career path. As a political scientist, I am acutely aware of the fact that my discipline's classic question—Who gets what, when, how?—is just as applicable to our own scholarly production as it is to our research subjects.[2] I first provide background on my research project; I then explore the dynamics I experienced while attempting to gain access to the communities I studied and then the dilemmas I faced while trying to make use of my research.

THE WASTE IS A TERRIBLE THING TO MIND: MY RESEARCH PROJECT

Like most social scientists, when I try to tell the strangers I sit next to on airplanes what I study, my answers get long and confusing. This is probably due to the fact that social science subfields are now so numerous and narrowly focused that they must be combined to answer any complex social question. I am a political scientist who specializes in environmental policy, social movements, and U.S. state and local politics. More specifically, I study variation in community responses to the siting of low-level radioactive waste disposal facilities.

I have found that my captive airline audience tends to assume that the inspiration for my research came from a passionate interest in radioactive waste. Most people, including some of my professors in graduate school, assumed that I started on the topic as either an antinuclear activist or a nuclear-industry professional. But I did not follow either of these paths to my research topic; my interest grew purely out of an academic curiosity in social movement behavior. I wanted to answer the question of why, when given the same grievances, communities vary in both their frequency and strategy of collective opposition. Thus, my chosen topic of study was the end result of a search for a universe of communities that had faced an identical environmental grievance. I think many graduate students start with a personal interest in a topic and then search for compelling academic questions to fit that interest. I latched onto an academic question, chose a topic that fit that question, and only developed a personal interest in the topic during the course of my research. Of course, the places I chose to look for my universe of cases were determined by previous interest and training in U.S. politics and environmental policy. But the key point remains that I did not have to cultivate academic relevance during my research, but instead a personal passion for my topic.

Here, then, is the topic I adopted. In 1980, Congress took the unprecedented step of devolving responsibility for the disposal of commercially generated low-level radioactive waste (LLRW) to state governments and regional compacts. In the late 1980s and early 1990s states and regional compacts identified twenty-five different counties as candidate sites for LLRW disposal facilities. Although opposition was nearly universal in these affected communities, they varied in the frequency of collective acts of opposition mustered, the type of collective action undertaken, and the policy success they achieved. After providing a policy history that explained the 1980 devolution, I sought to explain this variation across twenty-one of the affected communities.

I did not originally conceive of this project as a fieldwork exercise in these communities. I began this project in the solitary confinement of state libraries across the country. This was going to be a quantitative project based on event analysis taken from local newspaper accounts, data on social capital culled from old phonebooks and civic organization archives, public meeting content drawn from state archives, and census data. I viewed over a thousand reels of microfilm before I met a single person in one of these affected communities. I had social movement theories to test.

The test results were disappointing and would not alone provide the basis for a dissertation; it was time to meet some people in these communities. But something besides methodological necessity was pushing me into the field. By reading years of local newspapers for each affected community I had developed a personal passion for my research topic to match my academic curiosity. I was beginning to feel like a member of these communities without ever having set foot in town.

Of course, I had read all about each community's struggle with the LLRW issue. I had read news accounts about the first organizational meetings, the civil disobedience events, and the lobbying trips to state legislatures. I had also followed the developing letter-to-the-editor contributions of numerous individuals. I knew the names and faces of both civic leaders and involved citizens. I wanted to meet the woman in Allegeny County, New York who organized an ice cream social/gun raffle to raise money for the LLRW opposition, and the man in Cortland County, New York, who organized a demolition derby car-jumping competition for the same purpose. I was fascinated by the pig-kissing fund raisers in Nebraska communities and the pig pickin' barbecue fundraisers in North Carolina. I also found it hard to separate news of the LLRW issue from other community events. I read about crop reports, local United Way campaigns, dances at the the local Grange halls, homecoming courts, high school football championships, and elementary school cafeteria menus.

At the same time as I was discovering the richness of these communities, I was also reading the reports of state LLRW siting agents, who referred to these places as "backward," "depressed," "disadvantaged," "uneducated," "unenlightened," and even "ignorant." Although state policy always dictated that LLRW sites be chosen according to the physical characteristics of geology and hydrology, it was clear that the site selection professionals were heavily basing their site selection on socioeconomic characteristics. A National Research Council review of the New York LLRW siting process found "technical performance and socioeconomic criteria were combined inappropriately during Candidate Area Identification."[3] The Illinois Department of Nuclear Safety used socioeconomic data to select a candidate site before completing a technical analysis of the physical site. I found a confidential site selection report issued by a contractor for the state of North Carolina that described favorable sites with the comments "trailers everywhere" and "distressed county," while describing unfavorable sites as "affluent."

Before I had uncovered this information I had taken the selection of these sites as a given. I had wrongly assumed that the sites shared geological and hydrological characteristics that served as a control for my universe of cases. However, the stark contrast between my own growing affinity for these communities and the callous abuse of these communities by site selection professionals led me to augment my research project. Rather than confining my political science research to essentially the question of who gets organized, when, and how, I expanded it to explore who gets stuck with radioactive waste, when, and how. I applied a quantitative environmental justice analysis, which revealed that more than two-thirds of the LLRW candidate sites demonstrated significant environmental justice concerns on the income dimension as defined by the Environmental Protection Agency. I probed the issue further by interviewing former site selection contractors and involved elected officials who confessed that the site selection was essentially a political exercise in identifying communities that were not likely to oppose an LLRW site.

The environmental justice concerns across these cases did more than create an additional avenue of academic inquiry; they tapped a deep personal affinity within me for these affected communities. State officials' callous disregard for the health of working-class communities reminded me of a poignant moment from my childhood in Buffalo, New York. When I was six years old, my parents and I drove through the neighboring city of Love Canal after the residents had been evacuated to escape the seepage of approximately two hundred toxic chemicals from an abandoned dump into their homes. Although my family was not directly affected by the Love Canal disaster, the image of this abandoned working-class neighborhood very similar to my own, a fifteen-minute drive away, had a haunting effect on me as a child. I knew that the Niagara Falls municipal government had knowingly purchased the contaminated land and cleared it for development as a school and residential neighborhood. Later, in the midst of my graduate research, I started to see the LLRW affected-communities as similar to my own working class-area in western New York. The politics of why I write had become personal: my detached academic objectives were now joined by a personal affinity for the communities I was studying. What, when, and how I write was now influenced by more than academic curiosity. I wanted to meet the people affected by the proposed LLRW sites on both an academic and a personal level.

EXPRESSING WHY I WRITE AND GAINING ACCESS

The fact that I had linked my academic interest in these affected communities with a newly developed personal interest did not mean, however, that I would gain an invitation to the next community pig roast. Obviously I had to cultivate the trust of key community members in order to gain access. While plenty of practical guides to fieldwork offer tips on building trust and gaining access, my experience has taught me that this process is idiosyncratic: the response one draws from the community to one's request for access and information is largely determined by prior experiences the community has had with curious outsiders.

I was never the first outsider seeking access to study these affected communities. In a few exceptional instances I followed a journalist or an academic who had provided the community members with a positive experience. Most often, I followed on the heels of someone who, at best, had simply misunderstood the community or, at worst, had taken advantage of it. For example, I found myself following state and national environmental groups who sought to help some of these communities organize opposition but ended up insulting the local leaders by mistakenly casting the struggle as antinuclear rather than pro-rural identity and property rights. I also once followed a shady door-to-door saleswoman who was attempting to sell aura photographs to people she deemed to be antinuclear activists.

While these experiences certainly made members of the affected communities suspicious of outsiders interested in the LLRW issue, the worst outsiders I had to follow into these communities were the state officials and consultants working on LLRW site selection. These site selection professionals left the communities in which they worked seething with hostility toward curious outsiders. Twelve years before I attempted to gain access to an affected community in North Carolina, a consultant for the Chem-Nuclear company working for the state used her research on LLRW candidate sites to write a masters thesis titled "Incentives, Compensation, and Other Magic Tricks," designed to serve as a guide to identifying acquiescent communities. Some communities even endured surveillance by state and federal law enforcement officials. When I was writing letters of introduction to affected community members, in my own mind I had clearly distinguished my reasons for writing from those of my predecessors. Yet this distinction was not at all obvious to the community members. This is why, even ten years after the most intense periods of struggle over the LLRW issue, I was met with questions as serious as whether or not I was a federal agent.

I found three things helpful in gaining trust and ultimately access into the community: (1) being aware of the community's past experiences with interested outsiders; (2) demonstrating personal interest in the community and local knowledge; and (3) making a time commitment to the community. Each of these is at least in part an answer to the "why I write" question, an expression of why I am interested in this topic.

First, my own awareness of some of the community's negative encounters with outsiders helped me distinguish myself and make it clear that the reason I was writing was not to exploit the community. I had read the reports of the site selection professionals, which revealed environmental justice concerns as well as egregious planning errors. In one case a state siting official surveyed the wrong site on the wrong road. The correct site would have dislocated less than five households; the site he surveyed would have dislocated nearly one hundred households. Nevertheless, the site he mistakenly surveyed became the preferred site. Of course, none of the environmental justice concerns or planning errors were news to the affected communities; they knew far more about these transgressions than I did. These were, after all, the source of their grievances. But my awareness of these transgressions, which I communicated in my initial phone conversations with community members, helped to distinguish me from the outsiders who had committed them. And my willingness to learn more about issues like this gave community members an opportunity to inform me on their own terms. When I brought up the surveying error in phone conversations with the community members most affected by it, I found the tenor of the conversation changed immediately. These people had attempted in vain for years to get the site selection professionals to admit this planning mistake. By simply acknowledging the surveying mistake I obtained some common ground with the community, some distinction between myself and the outsiders who had made that mistake, and multiple offers for pickup truck tours of the two sites in question.

Second, the personal interest and connection to these affected communities I had developed while in solitary library confinement served me well as I contacted community members. I could establish the fact that I was writing out of a genuine and personal interest in the community. The site selection professionals who preceded me demonstrated no interest in learning what these affected communities valued. In fact, the reports these professionals produced were designed to convince state officials that these candidate sites hosted nothing of value that would be damaged by the LLRW disposal facility. In contrast, pouring over years of local newspapers not only gave me an appreciation for what each of these communities had to offer, but also helped me identify these communities with my own small town, working-class roots in western New York.

By far the most common questions I was asked during my initial telephone conversations with community members were, "Why are you interested in this?" and "What do you know about this community?" The first question was often framed in a way that asked for my biography. The second question was sometimes framed in a way that queried whether I myself was from a rural community, and other times it was asked in order to quiz me on my knowledge of local information. I could not claim to be from a rural community, but I could relay the connection I perceived between my childhood experience at Love Canal and the experiences of these affected communities. I could also express my appreciation for these communities, which had grown out of local newspaper stories.

In one memorable case in the southern United States I headed off a chilly reception by a particularly suspicious community leader by turning the conversation toward this community's state championship football team. Months earlier I had found myself distracted by stories of this football team's improbable triumph over teams from much more affluent and prosperous counties. When I mentioned the team's undefeated record I not only displayed my appreciation for the community's most salient point of pride, but also uncovered the community's most powerful resource in their opposition to the LLRW disposal facility.

The woman with whom I was speaking responded to the football team topic by declaring, "We have a powerhouse football team. We can beat any team in the state and those kids go on to college, to serve in the armed forces, and to become leaders in the community. We're not a bunch of yahoos. Their success shows how we value character in this community." She went on to tell me that "more people come together for those football games than anything else" and that the LLRW opposition movement undertook their first organizational efforts at a game, used the booster club as an organizational resource, and had the players in uniform take part in demonstrations as a symbolic resource. In this case my interest in the football team put many of the interviewees I spoke with at ease and demonstrated my sincere appreciation for their community.

In other instances, a local knowledge of small-town politics proved useful. In another southern community a sheriff had held office for more than fifty years and exercised influence over almost every aspect of local life. I had followed his activity in the local papers and read revealing profiles of his tenure in the regional papers. I knew that the sheriff intimidated most community members. As one interviewee eventually conceded, "We were always afraid of ending up in the river." I always conveyed my awareness of the sheriff's influence and expressed my intent to work discretely and diplomatically in the community.

Third, and perhaps most important, my willingness to commit significant amounts of time building relationships in the community helped forge relationships that enriched my life as well as my research. Many community members told me that they weren't willing to conduct interviews over the telephone. After my initial contacts with a letter and follow-up telephone call, I knew I had to commit to spending time in these communities. One interviewee told me that "we're not like city people, we need to get to know you first, look you in the eye, and maybe even share a meal with you before we talk. We want to know what you're like." Consequently, I spent much more time walking the fence with people, drinking lemonade, sharing meals, and talking about everything but the LLRW issue than I did interviewing people. In one case I spent more than three hours of small talk with a farming couple while they introduced me to their domesticated raccoons, groundhogs, and coyote before our conversation could move to their involvement in the LLRW disposal siting process. The hospitality that I often experienced was also a kind of interview conducted by the community members to determine if I could indeed be trusted. At the same time that these people were feeding me and sometimes even providing a place for me to stay with my dog, they were attempting to figure out why I write. Opening myself up to this familiarization process not only demonstrated my goodwill; it turned the research process into a human enterprise as well as an academic one.

Who gains access, and when and how in communities such as these? Individuals who have gained the trust of community members gain access only when they have exhibited a good-faith commitment to the community by distinguishing themselves from those that would exploit the community, demonstrating a personal interest in and knowledge of the community, and committing time getting to know community members on a personal level. The personal interest I had developed during the archival phase of my research served me well. Although my passion for the academic questions that drove my research were important to me, this reason for writing would not have been enough on its own to gain access to these affected communities. Only a genuine personal interest in these communities and a serious commitment to learning about all aspects of local life could build the necessary trust with my interviewees. Most people do not like to be studied or considered objects of academic research, particularly if previous curious outsiders have exploited them. But many people do like to teach others what they have learned from their experiences and are more than willing to share with outsiders who have demonstrated a personal interest.

DECIDING WHAT TO WRITE

In addition to learning the reasons for my interest in LLRW, most of my interviewees wanted to know what I was going to do with the information I obtained. I was still wrestling with this question of what to write long after the completion of my research. On one level, the answer to this question was clearly stated on my human subjects consent form, which each of my interviewees had to sign. This form warned, "You should realize that the information you provide in the interview is likely to appear in publication." I then explained that this research was the basis for my dissertation, which I hoped to publish in the future either as a series of articles or a book.

None of my interviewees ever objected to my dissertation or academic publication endeavors. Some requested that I send them a copy or place a copy in the local public library, and others wanted assurances that I would not write reports for the nuclear industry. But many wondered why I was not going to do more with this research. As one interviewee said, "You've got an awful lot of people's efforts here, including your own, to have it end up in some reports only professors will read." I'm not sure what other publication outlets he had in mind, but many interviewees seemed to want me to use my research to create a local history documenting their opposition to LLRW. One interviewee even tried to express his idea of my work by comparing it to that of John and Alan Lomax, the father and son team that began in the 1930s to record American folk songs for the Library of Congress. While I don't pretend to keep company with these American icons, I do take the point that my research might have some applications beyond the narrow academic universe I originally envisioned.

When I finished my fieldwork I was struck by the fact that the scope of my dissertation project captured such a small amount of the information I gained in these affected communities. The word-count data alone from my interview transcripts and my manuscript are very revealing: less than one percent of the words from my interview transcripts actually ended up in the manuscript. From this perspective the answer to the question, "What are you going to do with this information?" is, "Not much."

While I started to pursue local history projects on specific cases, I also started searching for some additional outlets for my research that would fulfill the responsibilities I felt to both academia and the communities from which I learned so much. The additional outlet I discovered was not writing at all, but teaching. I have found a meaningful venue for much of the information I gained during my research—but did not use in my academic writing—in the classroom.

The best example of information used in my newly discovered outlet is not from a LLRW opponent, but information I gleaned from a rural community member in central New York who actually supported the LLRW disposal facility. This man actually volunteered to sell his land to host the facility, sparking a tremendous amount of conflict in the local community. I used this situation and this man's story to add complexity to my students' understanding of environmental justice issues. Before I told the man's story, my students saw him in villainous terms as either a pawn of the state or a greedy landowner. I then revealed several key facts about his life. He lives on a failed dairy farm that has been in his family for more than two hundred years. It costs him more to produce milk than he can recover by selling it. He blames this situation on the decreasing consumption of milk and the increasing consumption of soda. He cannot afford to pay the taxes on his property, so he has taken an interstate trucking job hauling aluminum for soda cans. His only son recently died of leukemia. He has offered to sell a portion of his land to the state, so he can keep the remainder of his family farm.

These facts provided a personal yet broadening context for my students that emphasized larger economic justice issues while complicating any simple understanding of environmental justice. However, my lectures are not the only outlet that teaching provides. My students also greatly benefit from learning how to do their own community research and from coming to their own understanding of the interplay between academic and personal interests.

Yet, the greatest potential advantage of the classroom is that it can provide a forum for the exchange of ideas between community members and academia. Inviting community members to speak in my classes is the best marriage between my responsibilities as an academic and my responsibilities to the communities I study. As I have mentioned, most people do not like to be studied, but many people like to teach and share their experiences with others; the classroom can provide community members with an enjoyable and meaningful venue in which to do this. The students, and academia as a whole, greatly benefit from these visits from individuals who encourage us to pursue the most practical and applied aspects of our academic endeavors.

Using the classroom in this way can be thought of as an act of brokerage. In social-science jargon, brokerage is "the linking of two or more previously unconnected social sites by a unit that mediates their relations with one another and/or with yet other sites."[4] In my research on these affected communities, brokers were important individuals who in various instances linked previously disconnected racial or geographic factions of the community, or brought together citizen activists and government officials. This brokerage helped to explain both the frequency and type of collective action. Now I have started to view my own professional role as that of a broker, bringing together the too-often unconnected social sites of community members and academia. Writing alone will not achieve brokerage; the connection must be personal and reciprocal. Teaching provides opportunities for these kinds of connections.

I came to this realization while I was simultaneously finishing my dissertation and looking for a full-time academic position. I had three very different kinds of academic job opportunities: a research-centered position, a teaching-centered position, and a position that combined research and teaching with a community liaison role. I was familiar with the territory of the first two opportunities, yet I took the third—less conventional—option because I felt it would best allow me to pursue my newfound role as a broker. The job I accepted enables me to teach and conduct research on environmental policy, yet also encourages me to build bridges between the university and environmental stakeholders in the region.

This career decision and my affinity for this new job developed out of my own struggles with the "why I write" question. I began writing strictly out of academic curiosity, but developed a personal interest in the communities I researched, and this took me into the field and helped me cultivate meaningful relationships in these communities. I then realized that the politics of writing—what gets written, when, and how—is rather limiting. Members of the communities I studied helped me understand that scholarly writing alone may not be making the fullest use of the information I gather. I felt a need to creatively expand the application of my academic research. Identifying my professional role as that of a broker between the academy and the community is helping me fulfill this need.

14

WHY I DON'T WRITE

Erme C. Maula

It would seem simple to list all of the reasons of why I do not write. It seems like I always have a reason not to be writing, or at least not to be writing what I need to be writing. It is a vicious cycle. As a favor, and because I was ecstatic that someone from the field of nursing would be asked to present alongside other disciplines, I decided to put my "reasons" aside to be able to contemplate and articulate *why I don't write.*

In 2003, I was asked to present at the conference Why We Write: The Politics and History of Writing for Social Change. When I first heard this title, I giggled, as I often do, and said to myself that in my case it should be called Why I *Don't* Write. Folks may wonder why a nursing student would be presenting at a history conference. To me, it made perfect sense to combine the theme of the previous year's conference, History of Activism, History as Activism, with the necessity of the 2003 theme. Nurses, as many may or may not know, have often been effective advocates and quiet activists. Nurses have been around throughout history, observing, and creating change in ways that directly affect the lives of those around them—especially the sick. It was nurses such as Susie Walking Bear Yellowtail, who worked with the Indian Health Service from 1929 to 1931, who helped to end abuses such as the

sterilization of Native American women without their consent. Margaret
Sanger, another nurse, is the founder of the American birth control
movement. Adah Belle Samuel Thoms, one of the first African Americans
to hold a high-level position as president of the National Association of
Colored Graduate Nurses, worked to address issues of racism with nursing practice and training. Often, nurses are not looked to as academics,
although our work is scholarly and methodical. One of our downfalls,
however, is the historical documentation of the social change aspects of
our profession. *So, why don't I write about it?*

I have had many conversations with fellow colleagues working in
social justice, activism, advocacy, and academia about the need for
more connections among these fields. I have worked on endless coalitions, collaborations, and interdisciplinary teams to address the issues
we face when working with communities. I have spent years working
alongside women fighting to be recognized, not for them necessarily,
but for their brothers and sisters who could not be vocal. I realize that
it has been a privilege to integrate advocacy into my work and academic life. I also realize that it is a privilege to have been able to work in
and out of academia, understanding and living the realities and conflicts between the two worlds. In theory, these two worlds are working
toward creating a better society, although they often collide. This privilege often becomes a burden when trying to live fully in both worlds.
So, why don't I write?

As doctoral students, we all know that time is precious. The irony is
that I spend just as much time thinking about how I do not have any
time to do the things I need to do. I always, however, find time to do
what is important to me: chatting online, having coffee with friends,
making dinner, or watching a movie. Because it may seem silly that
these are my *important* things, I feel the need to justify them. I feel that
in order to do the work we nurses do—the sharing of intellectual discourse, activism, and advocacy—we need to fuel our souls with those
things that keep us going. In the midst of engaging in activities to influence history, I think that we need to come back to reality every now
and then, and just *be.*

When asked what I do, I often respond, "I am an advocate's
advocate." I try to pave the way and support the work of others,
especially those striving for social justice. I like to hang out in the
background, bring coffee and treats, drive people to where they need to
go, and be a compassionate ear when needed. This allows me to be
present at vulnerable times for those trying to make change, providing
me with an "in" to ensure my own agenda of creating a critical thinking,
social-justice-minded, integrated world. From a nursing philosophy,

I holistically integrate the physical, psychological, spiritual, emotional, and often financial realms of advocates. This is a view of nurses and nursing advocates that does not get printed on nursing school promotional material. Who wants a nurse that is selfish in her own agenda and doesn't just want to just "help people"? I often find the need to document this aspect of nursing, but writing has always been my downfall.

WHY DON'T I WRITE? FIRST, IT IS DUE TO PHYSICAL EXHAUSTION.

I am too busy conducting eroticizing safer sex workshops, talking over dinner and educating women on their options on how to give birth, flirting with Dorothy Allison to get her view on how the Internet affects lesbian health issues and community organizing, researching which digital camera would be best to document the oral histories of Asian and Pacific Islander women in the HIV/AIDS movement, and talking to the guy on the plane who is flying out from San Francisco to market his paint, which is used for bombs and planes.

My energy is spent mentoring a young photographer who is conflicted between doing civil disobedience or documenting the antiwar protests in Philadelphia, getting her to understand the larger worldview and need for those photos over her being in jail.

My day is spent consoling a burnt-out community activist, buying her dinner and sending her flowers, offering her hope and reminding her of her purpose and the impact on the world she is making.

My time is spent in at least three major cities on planes, trains, and automobiles. It is spent with two national networks getting the women from New York to hear the issues of women in Palau, when most people can't even find it on a map. It is spent raising the necessity of building individual capacity around issues of oppression before writing letters to the U.S. Congress as a coalition of individuals. It is spent looking for children's books for my two nephews that will teach them, as well as their parents, about acceptance and love as they are read at bedtime. It is spent talking to my mother, who is surviving a cancer diagnosis, and then daydreaming about a real vacation.

And all of this in the past week.

It takes a lot of energy to write. As an advocate, my mind is constantly racing to keep up with the messages that I am being bombarded with throughout the day. I quickly analyze each of these messages, integrate them into my foundational philosophy of nursing, and then interpret all of these messages in a way that makes sense to me, and then translate my findings for others, at all levels of understanding. My mind then needs to deconstruct each word, assess which level of understanding where someone may fall, and then readjust my findings to fit into that mold. All of this is done in the split second I have when noticing a billboard on the side of the road. It is exhausting.

So, take this constant bombardment and burden of analysis, and add it to the need to physically be in several places to address specific aspects of society's messages while absorbing more messages en route, and still needing to eat and sleep—it makes me tired. And then I'm supposed to write it all down? Are you starting to see why I don't write?

I realize that this is not a unique perspective of activism. I find that my fellow activists are also challenged with juggling their advocacy alongside their writing. Many of us feel the need to document what we see, what we think, and what we think needs to be done. The problem is that we just don't have the time or resources to write. Those resources come in many forms, but sometimes we find ourselves at a loss. I realize that this creates a biased historical view of our work. I find that those who have the time and resources to write are the ones who are not burdened with other aspects of their lives. Perhaps they are well-adjusted; perhaps they do not have student loans or a car payment. Perhaps they have good credit and a fast computer. This leaves an interesting predicament since as advocates, we fight against the present documented history, but cannot write a better version. Who decides what goes into the history books, who are seen as experts, and whose view is "right"? Those who do write, and get published, are often those who are not in the middle of the movement. My fear is that when someone comes back to look for these documents that do not exist, they are left to find only those written by those of privilege. Who has written about oral histories of Asian and Pacific Islander women within the HIV/AIDS movement? Who has documented the story of seventy-year-old Suki Terada Ports, who has been fighting her whole life, or twenty-eight-year-old Joslyn Maula, who resigned from her job as an executive director of an Asian and Pacific Islander HIV/AIDS organization because she did not have enough support?

Ports was instrumental in forcing New York City to address the issues of people of color, especially women, around HIV/AIDS. She was among the first to vocalize and fight for the needs of communities in New York as well as throughout the United States, helping to establish organizations such as the National Minorities AIDS Council. She continues even today, with more energy than I have ever had, as the executive director of the Family Health Project in New York City. My biological sister, Joslyn Maula, joined the fight as a social worker who gained the understanding of social justice and its impact on Asian and Pacific Islander communities in Washington, D.C. From the work of such heroic activists to the everyday trials of my own sister's struggles within a nonprofit organization, the work of activists goes unnoticed and underappreciated. But who writes about them? The result is that history becomes skewed, and we need to skew it into our own reality for it to make the difference we want.

As I get older, the strains of decreased metabolism are taking its toll on my body. I am no longer able to pull all-nighters, go without eating and sleeping, or travel as frequently as I once did. I find that I need to go to the gym to relieve stress, increase my cardiac output, and get in touch with "current events" as I watch CNN and old episodes of *The West Wing*. It has become not only a luxury but a necessity to take this time for myself throughout the week. It keeps my blood pressure from rising to the astronomical levels they were when I was solely doing advocacy work. Now, the only way I can continue doing advocacy work is to engage in other activities—self-care, as it is often referred to—to survive. My health just cannot take it. I cannot take the headaches, the anxiety, the heartaches, the lack of sleep, the high blood pressure, and the hunger associated with doing advocacy work. I cannot take the illnesses acquired on planes, trains, and buses. But I continue to do the work, and continue now to write about it.

I have found that living is exhausting. Being "on" to address the needs of others is exhausting. Being able to constantly conduct political, social, and spiritual analyses on the world around me is exhausting. Having to fit in self-care time in the gym takes away from my day, and although I leave feeling better than I did when I first walked in, it leaves me less time to do my work. Although I consider myself young, I feel that I have an old soul, exhausted before I started, my physical body exhausted by living.

WHY DON'T I WRITE? AN EASY SECOND ANSWER WOULD BE FOR LACK OF RESOURCES.

It takes simple resources to write—paper, pens, a desk. I find, however, that it takes more than that. It takes a computer with broadband Internet access, a pair of new bifocal glasses to assist in reading the computer screen, a desk big enough to hold all the different piles of papers I am working on, good coffee that I have become accustomed to drinking, a cell phone to schedule meetings, and a house big enough to give me room to write, live, sleep, and entertain. It takes a combination scanner/printer/fax machine, and all of the computer accessories to make my writing easier. It is not like the Jack Kerouac way of writing in a notebook while traveling anymore: writing these days takes a mobile modem to be able to blog online instantaneously while participating in a demonstration or conducting lectures on the road. I need to come up with money for a gym membership, car insurance, train and plane tickets, and rent. I need to eat healthy food, drink coffee in shops while people-watching and working, and do my laundry every now and then. I need to pay parking tickets I received while running into a store to buy a new book, picking up research articles that were sent via interlibrary loan, or picking up my prescription for the antidepressants I started for symptoms of post-traumatic stress disorder after starting my doctoral program. So, writing takes money and resources.

I never thought of myself as a frivolous person. I was always somewhat of a minimalist and grew up with immigrant parents. After attending an Ivy League institution for my undergraduate studies (honestly not realizing that I was not applying to a state school), I found that I had what sociologists call "cultural collateral." I had the language, desires, know-how, and eventually a degree to show that I knew how it was to have resources, but I did not necessarily have the finances to back it up.

Perhaps this is where my paralyzing concept of being a fraud started. Although I was a regular traditional student, I never felt that I fit in. I had classmates around me with their new computers (I had to use computer labs), seasonal wardrobes (I was happy in my hand-me-downs and nonfashionable clothes), extravagant spring break vacations (I always planned on going "home" to my parents), new cars (I did not have a car and relied on public transportation), and no need for financial aid (I worked two or three jobs at any one time). I lived and studied beside them, not ever thinking to stop and ask if they thought I was "one of them." Looking back, I wonder what they thought of me; I wonder if they thought I was any different. My experience of having immigrant parents, growing up in the South, being a child of someone in the military, and being subjected to (but benefiting from) the concept of being a "model minority" helped to establish who I am today, but made me different from those around me. So, resources come in many forms, but it's the financial ones that I find myself often lacking.

WHY DON'T I WRITE? A THIRD REASON IS COMPETING PRIORITIES.

Our own personal identity is often in conflict with the work that we are doing. I am a queer, Asian woman; a teacher and a student; a sister and a daughter; an advocate and a nurse. Which do you address first? Am I a woman first and then Asian? Am I queer and then a student? Am I a teacher and a nurse? Am I an activist and then a revolutionary?

I am also an incest survivor, a trained rape crisis counselor, and a researcher. Can we really prioritize this list? It would be a very Western practice to do so. Another approach would be to weave these identities together into something similar to a double helix to create the foundational blueprint of my being. The list of identities can go on and on.

We are all faced with competing identities on several levels. Individually, we are often asked to identify and choose between these identities. This in turn forces us to neglect an aspect of ourselves when interacting in certain groups. For instance, if I am with a group of Filipino students, will I also be perceived as queer at the same time as Filipina? I do not feel that I am in conflict with my various identities; it is just a phenomenon that forces us to make this quick decision, assess the situation again, and decide what is important to focus on within a discussion and conversation. We teach students to be goal oriented, and I stress the importance of assessing each situation individually, throwing it into the context of a larger worldview, and then decide what is best for oneself at that moment.

And then there are the consequences of prioritizing. What do you do if you choose one aspect to publicly advocate for, but then want to bring up other issues? What happens if you "out" the issues fought within communities, when the outside world never suspected that they existed?

Because of my work in HIV/AIDS as an Asian and Pacific Islander advocate, I'm faced with the conflict of airing "dirty laundry" through my writing—bringing light to the conflicts that exist within my communities, often hidden within the invisibility. How do you put into words the sexism, racism, and classism that exist within a movement that is trying to appear as working in solidarity? How do you talk about male partners of Asian wives who take part in extramarital sexual activities with both men and women? How do you talk about the domestic abuse, the mental health issues, and the extra stresses put on Asian families? How do you advocate for the need for help for a community that prides itself on being self-sufficient?

Asians are often referred to as the "model minority." Many people, especially those in education, fall into the guise of thinking that they treat everyone the same. There are those assumptions—and I teach that they are okay to have—that we bring to the table or classroom. I spend a lot of time in my workshops talking about these assumptions. Many "diversity" facilitators will tell you to "leave your assumptions at the door." I, on the other hand, tell you to take those assumptions and bring them into the elevator with you. A quick exercise to try when you cannot identify your assumptions is to close your eyes and stand in an empty elevator. Have the doors open, and have "that person" walk in. Have the doors close, and then think about what you are seeing, feeling, and experiencing during your elevator ride with this person, who can make you feel good or bad. Either way, you have created the image based on your assumptions. Those are what you need to embrace, and figure out what to do with in your life.

So, where is the conflict? Well, there is a part of us that wants to be seen as working in solidarity, rising above conflict, harmoniously advocating the same issues. Then there is the reality of oppressions that exists within each movement. There are always different levels to acknowledge within groups. I went with Lesbians for a Better America (LBA) to listen to Mary Frances Berry and Angela Davis speak, ironically on the first day of the second term of George W. Bush. I felt that it was symbolic on this day to be with these women, Berry and Davis, but also to be with my sisters in LBA. Berry and Davis both spoke about the competing priorities and identities of women within movements. They spoke about the need to honor the interconnectedness of identities. They spoke about the black movement *and* the women's movement, and the issues that men, especially, had with integrating the two. I have felt the struggle of Asian men integrating an Asian and Pacific Islander movement with the women's movement.

How do you write about the arguments and hurt feelings you have as a woman, when working with men that are not sensitive to gender dynamics though you all are seen to be working in solidarity? I am often in this quandary when working within coalitions. Who can you trust and not trust? Who is really an ally, and who is really just out for himself? What is going on in someone's life to change her agenda—hidden or not—and how will that evolve? Who is learning to be politically savvy? Who already is? And who thinks that they are, but are not yet?

Another competing priority, as well as a consequence to writing and vocalizing issues, is the reflection it has on one's family. Topics such as sex and drugs may seem to be normalized in the United States; however, they remain among the many topics still considered taboo within the Asian and Pacific Islander community. It is okay to have undocumented workshops and talks about culturally taboo topics such as sexual orientation and incest, but I am not sure about the possibility of my parents or my aunties seeing my name attached to a workshop titled Eroticizing Safer Sex for Lesbians. What would that say about me? Do I care what other people think? Does it matter that I am directly addressing topics that are forbidden to discuss in my own home and in the homes of my relatives? Will there be any backlash toward my parents and family? It is one thing to put oneself in the line of attack, but another to place one's unknowing parents and loved ones on the line. I have found that I needed to be direct with my parents about the work that I do. We have normalized it for them—normalized the idea that we talk about S-E-X, and use terms like *anal sex, cunnilingus, butt-banger,* and *condoms* on a regular basis.

Obviously wanting to preserve "traditional culture" as well as addressing the issues neglected within that same culture is contradictory at best. These competing priorities around identity and social issues affect my writing in three ways: (1) in my concern for the well-being of my family and loved ones who may become targets as a result of my writings; (2) I'm too busy vocalizing the need to interconnect these priorities, offering a different model to use when addressing each of them; and (3) where would I hope to start?

WHY DON'T I WRITE? FOURTH, BECAUSE OF EDUCATIONAL PARALYSIS.

As a graduate student I have found myself paralyzed. Trying to survive in an institution that I believe is hostile and trying to make me fail is paralyzing. It is exhausting being in an institution where I don't feel like I belong or have a right to be there, yet feeling like my ideas are valid, and where no one knows about my field of research but still can't wait to own whatever I produce. Being in an institution where I am surrounded by women, but few are actually feminist is paralyzing.

I also find it paralyzing to watch dynamics in the classroom. In one of my doctoral classes, we were arranged in a circle for discussion every week that we met. The whole semester was spent with all of the Asian international students sitting one after the other, followed by the one American-born Asian, one Hispanic student, one African-American student, and then all of the white students completing the circle on another side. Do you not see a problem with this? The people of color all noticed it; but those not in this group were ignorant to the arrangement. When I questioned the professor about it, she denied that it existed, therefore denying my experience in the class. Being told that you are invisible in the code that people often use is paralyzing. This paralysis spreads to my writing, which then takes on these internalized oppressive ideas: It's not good enough; you can't write well; you aren't smart enough; your research is not as important. I realize that I am acknowledging that I know these messages are false. However, when presented in a classroom setting, it becomes paralyzing enough to hinder writing about it.

There are the reasons I *need* to believe so that I can write. I *should* write because I *need* to be a voice for those who can't, or to write in place of someone else who would be more at risk to have their name on paper. I *should* write because I *need* to document my personal experience so that future students won't find themselves also paralyzed. I *should* write because I *need* to document the history of women, especially Asian and Pacific Islander women, from our own perspective. I *should* write because I *need* to bring light to the real issues of isolated communities and give them substance in a medium that can be forwarded in an e-mail, published in a book, and used to lobby the U.S. Congress. I *should* write because I *need* to write so that my cousin in Kuwait will receive mail and know he is thought about and loved. I *should* write because I *need* to help end this war, and document the audacity of the current administration. I *should* write because I *need* to teach my nephews about the world through my eyes and my realities. I *should* write because I *need* to create research so that culturally appropriate interventions can be "scientifically based." I *should* write because I *need* to document the history of the communities I am creating, providing insight into a unique worldview. I *should* write because I *need* to write as a form of therapy, writing for the sake of writing, not writing for the sake of earning something. I *should* write because I *need* to combat the taboos of my communities, especially around sex and sexuality; death and illness; lesbian, gay, bisexual, and transgender issues; patriarchy; rape and incest; and mental health. I *should* write because I *need* to create the dialogue around access to correct information, critical thinking, and the need for accurate history to be taught in our schools. I *should* write because I *need* to write, as I am smart, intelligent, "worth it," and important, and my views need to be heard. And finally, I *should* write because I *need* to write so that I can say I am one of a very few, or likely the first Asian dyke to graduate from the University of Pennsylvania School of Nursing with a Ph.D.

These are my thoughts on why I don't write. I really don't have any good excuses. I do hope that I have given you a snapshot of what it is like to be burdened with the desire to address social justice issues in society from a nursing perspective. I hope that I have made you sympathetic to the movements that need your attention. I hope that I have inspired you to fund my research, support other advocates, and to move yourself toward becoming a revolutionary in whatever form you find yourself to be. We don't all need to be Che Guevara, but we need to acknowledge that through our actions in our everyday lives we create change. It is in writing about that change that others can learn and grow. It is our responsibility to take up the burden, united in solidarity.

NOTES

INTRODUCTION

1. Marc Block, *The Historian's Craft* (1953); reprint, New York: Vintage, 1964).
2. David Thelan, "The Nation and Beyond: Transnational Perspectives on United States History," *Journal of American History* 86, no. 3 (December 1999): 967.

CHAPTER 2

1. It was probably just as great an influence on my thinking that the Harvard men I knew who won fellowships to study abroad were given substantially more money than I was. Further, women were not eligible to compete for the Rhodes Scholarships, the Marshall Scholarships, or other prestigious fellowships.
2. Indeed, when I was applying to study history at Princeton University, I was told by a distinguished woman historian that when she sent her application to Princeton in the 1960s, they forwarded it to Bryn Mawr College for her—suggesting she might be happier doing graduate work in history there. This was the kind of crippling condescension female academics faced during this era. Instead, she was admitted to Harvard, won the Bancroft Prize, and has taught at an Ivy League institution ever since.
3. Again, at my particular institution (Princeton), and in my department (history), this eventually resulted in an investigation of sex discrimination in the matter of funding, qualifying exams, and distributing teaching fellowships. The department reluctantly admitted that they were not consciously discriminating against women, just "favoring men," following intense deliberation.
4. It was a bit tricky when my department chair let me know that someone with my same name had recently published a piece called "Zombies in Heat."
5. Aspects of this topic are examined elsewhere in this volume, in the elegant essay by Jill Lepore.
6. Certainly my husband's career as an architect, with art and commerce in an equally conflicted imbalance, has its own baggage, as well.
7. If someone has been working more than a decade on a project, a manuscript that does not take archival research but requires intellectual discipline, then clearly the focus and energy has shifted from *writing* to *writer's block*, which is something that befalls nearly every professional writer. However, we only feel comfortable confessing such an affliction in the past tense—with a few notable exceptions, such as that of author Fran Liebowitz.

8. At the same time, many colleges and universities offer scholars the alternative of teaching and training students, and scores of campus teachers devote themselves to their students—which many claim absorbs all their energies—in lieu of churning out articles or books. In theory, academic jobs are for those who are able to do both—to publish *and* remain fresh in the classroom. Sadly, the academy has been consumed in the past few decades by debates to reform a system where too many permanent appointments are held by those who do *neither*—the "dead wood" syndrome. Simultaneously, the American Historical Association and other professional organizations are considering lowering standards for tenure so that publication requirements are eased—a policy that would reflect what has essentially already taken place. In fairness, this is a response to shrinking opportunities for scholarly publication, university press cutbacks, and other developments as much as the "one-book wonder" syndrome.
9. However, most of us who write for a living are indeed weighed on just such scales—with the litmus test of sales figures weighted most heavily.

CHAPTER 3

1. Timothy Patrick McCarthy, "In My Brother's House: White Scholars and the Future of Black Studies," *Souls* 6, nos. 3–4 (2004): 55–65.

CHAPTER 4

1. Jennifer L. Morgan, *Laboring Women: Reproduction and Gender in New World Slavery* (Philadelphia: University of Pennsylvania Press, 2004), 181, 191, 133, 132.

CHAPTER 5

1. David Thelen, "The Nation and Beyond: Transnational Perspectives on United States History," *The Journal of American History* 86, no. 3 (December 1999): 967.
2. Dana L. Robert, "From Missions to Mission to Beyond Missions: The Historiography of American Protestant Foreign Missions since World War II," in *New Directions in American Religious History*, eds. Harry S. Stout and D. G. Hart (New York: Oxford University Press, 1997), 368.
3. Kim Il-Sung, "Chnch'e chakka yesulgadrege," in *Kim Il-Sung snjip* (Pyongyang, 1954), 3:244–245, quoted in Brian Myers, *Han Srya and North Korean Literature: The Failure of Socialism Realism in the DPRK* (Ithaca: Cornell East Asia Series, 1994), 77.
4. Peter Novick, *That Noble Dream: The "Objectivity Question" and the American Historical Profession* (Cambridge: Cambridge University Press, 1988).
5. Thomas Bender, introduction to *Rethinking American History in a Global Age* (Berkeley: University of California Press, 2002).
6. The J. William Fulbright Foreign Scholarship Board, Award Terms and Conditions: American Scholars and Student Awards to Korea, insert to letter of acceptance to author, March 2003.
7. The J. William Fulbright Foreign Scholarship Board, letter to author, March 13, 2003.
8. Charles Bright and Michael Geyer, "Where in the World Is America: The History of the United States in the Global Age," in *Rethinking American History in a Global Age*, ed. Thomas Bender, 66.
9. Prasenjit Duara, "Transnationalism and the Predicament of Sovereignty: China, 1900–1945," *The American Historical Review* 102, no. 4 (October 1997): 1030.

10. David A. Hollinger, *Postethnic America: Beyond Multiculturalism* (New York: Basic Books, 1995).
11. Horace Grant Underwood, *The Call of Korea: Political, Social, Religious* (New York: Fleming H. Revell Company, 1908), 34–35.
12. "History of the Taiku Mission," 1907, Presbyterian Church in the U.S.A. Board of Foreign Missions Secretaries' Files: Korea Mission, 1903–1972, RG 140, box 1, folder 3, Presbyterian Historical Society, Philadelphia, PA.
13. Mattie Ivey, "A New Missionary's First Sabbath," *The Korea Mission Field* (November 1905).
14. Horace Horton Underwood, II, "Fulbright: Information Handbook for Fulbright Grantees to Korea" (handout, Korean–American Education Commission, 2003), n.p.
15. *Ibid.*, n.p.
16. Ian Tyrrell, "Making Nations/Making States: American Historians in the Context of Empire," *The Journal of American History* 86, no. 3 (December 1999): 1043.
17. Bender, *Rethinking American History in a Global Age*, 12.

CHAPTER 6

1. David Oppenheim's Report on John Herbst, 26 April 1916, Box 30, Folder 11, Committee of Fourteen Records, Rare Books and Manuscript Division, New York Public Library (hereafter C14).
2. David Oppenheim's Report of 1 September 1916, Box 30, Folder 4, C14.
3. Ibid.
4. David Oppenheim's Report on the Little Irish Association Dance, 9 September 1916, Box 30, Folder 5, C14.
5. Natalie Sonnichsen, "Supplementary Report to November 19, 1913," Box 39, Folder V: "DSI Investigator's Reports (raw and edited): Sonnichsen," C14.
6. Kathy Peiss, *Cheap Amusements: Working Women and Leisure in Turn-of-the-Century New York* (Philadelphia: Temple University Press, 1986).
7. Peiss, 54.
8. Elizabeth Alice Clement, "Trick or Treat: Prostitution and Working-Class Sexuality in New York City, 1900–1932," Ph.D. dissertation, University of Pennsylvania, 1998, 5.
9. Clement 66. Emphasis added.
10. This investigator identifies himself as "L" on his reports. Henry is the name "L" uses for the bartender, which I believe was his real name.
11. L's Report on Avenel Hotel, addressed to Mr. Hooke, 8 July 1913, Box 28, Folder "1913," C14.
12. Ibid.
13. This conversation on 26 June 1913 established the friendly relationship evident in the July reports discussed in the beginning.
14. Report on Avenel, addressed to Mr. Hooke, 26 June 1913, Box 28, Folder 1913," C14.
15. Report on Avenel Hotel, addressed to Mr. Hooke, 8 July 1913, Box 28, Folder "1913," C14.
16. Ibid.

CHAPTER 7

1. Patricia J. Williams, *The Alchemy of Race and Rights: Diary of a Law Professor* (Cambridge, MA: Harvard University Press, 1991), 19. Sociologist Avery Gordon suggests that these elusive shapes are in fact ghosts, the complete yet uncompleted histories

that call for our scholarly and emotional attention; see Gordon, *Ghostly Matters: Haunting and the Sociological Imagination* (Minneapolis: University of Minnesota Press, 1997), chapter 1.

2. It's a little like Toni Morrison's idea that Africanism, apparently absent from the national literary canon, is in fact omnipresent. We look at the work of white people's hands, and, if we let ourselves, we find the shape of black bodies; see Morrison, *Playing in the Dark: Whiteness and the Literary Imagination* (Cambridge, MA: Harvard University Press, 1992).

3. Sadly, her nearby house is falling to ruin. Once lovely, it now sits boarded up, the yard littered with the debris cast from passers-by.

4. Cooper's life and writings offer good illustrations for my arguments, but it should be noted that her intimate life has been more closely scrutinized than those of most of her peers. Part of this stems from the scandal her relationship with John Love occasioned; see, for example, Mary Helen Washington, "Introduction," in Anna Julia Cooper, *A Voice from the South* (1892, reprint, New York: W. W. Norton, 1999), xxxv–xxxviii.

5. Cooper, *A Voice from the South*, 72; emphasis in the original.

6. For a helpful discussion of how to see the relationship between society, culture, and sexuality, see Ellen Ross and Rayna Rapp, "Sex and Society: A Research Note from Social History and Anthropology," in *Powers of Desire: The Politics of Sexuality*, eds. Ann Snitow, Christine Stansell, and Sharon Thompson (New York: Monthly Review Press, 1983), 51–73. This collection has been enormously influential for historians of intimacy and sexuality.

7. Many histories, of course, are only selectively hidden. As Anne Firor Scott has pointed out, sometimes it's not that things are invisible, but that they are invisible to us. It is crucial, then, to explore the ways that identity, race, gender, era, and politics limit our abilities to see and hear histories other than our own. See Scott, "Most Invisible of All: Black Women's Voluntary Associations," *Journal of Southern History* 56 (1990): 3–22.

8. Darlene Clark Hine, "Rape and the Inner Lives of Black Women in the Middle West: Some Preliminary Thoughts on Dissemblance," in *Unequal Sisters: A Multicultural Reader in U.S. Women's History*, ed. Vicki Ruiz and Ellen Carol Dubois (New York: Routledge, 1994): 342–47.

9. Fabius J. Haywood Papers, North Carolina State Archives, Raleigh.

10. Anna Julia Cooper, *Personal Recollections of the Grimké Family and the Life and Writings of Charlotte Forten Grimké* (privately published, 1951), in Charles Lemert and Esme Bahn, *The Voice of Anna Julia Cooper* (Lanham, Md.: Rowman and Littlefield, 1998): 310.

11. Ibid., 313.

12. The French phrase would have been common enough for her to have known it well; she could have found it in French in the writing of Alexandre Dumas, in English in the writing of William Makepeace Thackeray, or even embroidered in silk on a postcard, as it sometimes was.

13. Cooper, *Personal Recollections*, 312.

14. Part of my aim is to reclaim phrases lost, to reassert ownership of the sentimental, florid, and romantic. Now the stuff of bodice rippers, notions like "love's lunacy" or "undying attachment" could still have felt to Cooper like apt descriptions of her relationship with George. Historians need access to a broader field of stylistic choices.

15. Cooper, "Simon of Cyrene," reprinted in Louise Daniel Hutchinson, *Anna J. Cooper: A Voice from the South* (Washington, D.C.: Anacostia Neighborhood Museum and Smithsonian Institution Press, 1981), 180.

16. Cooper, *A Voice from the South*, 69–70.

17. This comes from an obituary she wrote for three former students, in which she spells out the difficulty facing activist black women in particular. Like most clippings in Cooper's scrapbook, a Standard Oil Company book into which she has pasted her own and others' articles right over the text, this obituary has neither date nor newspaper citation. Anna Julia Cooper Papers, Moorland-Spingarn Research Center, Howard University (henceforth AJC Papers, MSRC), Box 23-7, Folder 89.
18. AJC Papers, MSRC, Box 23-4, Folder 50.
19. AJC Papers, MSRC, Box 23-4, Folder 50; see also Box 23-4, Folder 55 for the flower sketch.
20. Darlene Clark Hine points out the dangers of the "myths of the superheroic"; see Hine, "'In the Kingdom of Culture': Black Women and the Intersection of Race, Gender, and Class in Black History," in *Speak Truth to Power: The Black Professional Class in United States History* (Brooklyn, NY: Carlson, 1996), 36.
21. For one example of how this might be done, see Phyllis Rose, *Parallel Lives: Five Victorian Marriages* (New York: Alfred A. Knopf, 1983).
22. Octavio Paz, "Between What I See and What I Say," in *A Tree Within*, trans. Eliot Weinberger (New York: New Directions, 1988), 4–5.

CHAPTER 8

1. Sean Wilentz, "America Made Easy," *The New Republic*, July 2, 2001.
2. Lawrence Stone, "The Revival of Narrative: Reflections on a New Old History," *Past and Present* 85 (1979): 3–24.
3. Peter Burke, "History of Events and the Revival of Narrative," in *New Perspectives on Historical Writing*, ed. Peter Burke (Cambridge: Polity Press, 1991), 233–248.
4. Alain Corbin, *The Life of an Unknown: The Rediscovered World of a Clog Maker in Nineteenth-Century France*, translated by Arthur Goldhammer (New York: Columbia University Press, 2001).
5. Jon Franklin, *Writing for Story: Craft Secrets of Dramatic Nonfiction* (New York: Plume, 1984), chapter 1.
6. Jill Lepore, *New York Burning: Liberty, Slavery, and Conspiracy in Eighteenth-Century Manhattan* (New York: Knopf, 2005).
7. Quotations in these scenes are taken from the original trial proceedings, published in 1744 by the New York Supreme Court Justice Daniel Horsmanden as *Journal of the Proceedings in the Detection of the Conspiracy* (New York, 1744). For a fuller discussion of Horsmanden's *Journal*, see Lepore, *New York Burning*, chapter 4.

CHAPTER 9

1. This essay was originally published in *Civil War History* 1, no. 4, © 2004 by The Kent University Press. Reprinted with permission from the publisher.
2. The most-often-quoted version of this remark—"It is well that war is so terrible—we should grow too fond of it"—is from Douglas Southall Freeman, *R. E. Lee: A Biography*, 4 vols. (New York: Charles Scribner's Sons, 1934–35), 2:462. But Freeman seems to have altered an earlier rendition of the statement: either "It is well this is so terrible! We should grow too fond of it!" from John Esten Cooke, *A Life of Gen. Robert E. Lee* (New York: D. Appleton, 1871), 184, or "It is well that war is so terrible, or we would grow too fond of it," from Edward Porter Alexander, *Military Memoirs of a Confederate: A Critical Narrative* (New York: Charles Scribner's Sons, 1907), 302. Gary Gallagher carefully traces this history and notes that Longstreet, to whom the remark was

made, never mentioned it in his own writings. See his *The Fredericksburg Campaign: Decision on the Rappahannock* (Chapel Hill: University of North Carolina Press, 1995) xiin1; Thomas L. Connelly, *The Marble Man: Robert E. Lee and His Image in American Society* (New York; Alfred Knopf, 1977). I am grateful to comments from many friends and colleagues who helped me think about why we love the Civil War: Lynn Hunt, Charles Rosenberg, Tony Horwitz, Edward Ayers, James McPherson, Yonatan Eyal, Michael Bernath, Peter Kolchin, Bertram Wyatt-Brown, Gabor Boritt, Homi Bhabha, Jeremy Knowles, and all the participants in the Huntington Library's Civil War conference in October 2003 and in the AHA Presidential Session in January 2004, where I delivered versions of this paper.

3. Benjamin quoted in *Richmond Enquirer*, Mar. 8, 1861; *DeBow's Review* 30 (Jan. 1861): 52; Higginson quoted in George M. Fredrickson, *The Inner Civil War: Northern Intellectuals and The Crisis of the Union* (New York: Harper & Row, 1965), 73. Because my focus in this essay is on the love of war, I have not discussed the voices opposing it.

4. Fredrickson, *Inner Civil War*, 75; *Richmond Enquirer*, June 29, 1861.

5. See, for example, Stephen Elliott, *God's Presence with Our Army at Manassas* (Savannah, GA: W. Thorne Williams, 1861); Elliott, *How to Renew Our National Strength* (Richmond, VA: MacFarlane and Fergusson, 1862); Alexander Gregg, *The Duties Growing Out of It and the Benefits to be Expected from the Present War* (Austin, TX: *The State Gazette*, 1861); T. L. De Veaux, *Fast-Day Sermon* (Wytheville, VA: D. A. St. Clair, 1864); John William Draper, *Thoughts on the Future Civil Policy of America* (New York: Harper, 1865), 251. One can find very similar statements on both sides at the outset of World War I. See Eric Leed, *No Man's Land: Combat and Identity in World War I* (Cambridge: Cambridge University Press, 1979).

6. Fredrickson, 80; *Richmond Enquirer*, June 29, 1861.

7. Earl J. Hess, "'Tell Me What the Sensations Are: The Northern Home Front Learns about Combat," in, *Union Soldiers and the Northern Homefront: Wartime Experiences, Postwar Adjustments*, eds. Paul A. Cimbala and Randall M. Miller (New York: Fordham University Press, 2002), 134–36; Oliver Wendell Holmes, "My Hunt After 'The Captain,'" *Atlantic* 10 (December 1862): 743; Gregory A. Coco, "Sightseers Flock to the Field," in *A Strange and Blighted Land: Gettysburg: The Aftermath of a Battle* (Gettysburg: Thomas Publications, 1995), 7. Sylvanus Cadwallader quoted in Charles Royster, *The Destructive War* (New York: Alfred Knopf, 1991), 248 (see in general chapter 6); illustration is "Maryland and Pennsylvania Farmers Visiting the Battle-Field of Antietam while the National Troops Were Burying the Dead and Carrying off the Wounded, Friday, Sept. 19," from *Frank Leslie's Illustrated*, October 19, 1862.

8. E. W. Locke quoted in Royster, *Destructive War*, 252; Mary Percy quoted in Hess, "'Tell Me . . . ,'" 123; Whitman quoted in Hess, "'Tell Me . . . ,'" 132–33.

9. Cyrus F. Boyd, *The Civil War Diary of Cyrus F. Boyd*, ed. Mildred Throne, (Millwood, NY: Kraus, 1977), 37; Ken Burns, "Four O'Clock in the Morning Courage," in *Ken Burns's The Civil War: Historians Respond*, ed. Robert Brent Toplin (New York: Oxford Univesrity Press, 1996), 159; James quoted in Fredrickson, *Inner Civil War*, 159; Ambrose Bierce, *A Sole Survivor: Bits of Autobiography*, eds. S. T. Joshi and David E. Schultz (Knoxville: University of Tennessee Press, 1998), 11.

10. William Blair, "The Quest for Understanding the Civil War," *Reviews in American History* 27 (September 1999): 421; Susan-Mary Grant, "Introduction," in *Legacy of Disunion: The Enduring Significance of the American Civil War*, eds. Grant and Peter Parish (Baton Rouge: Louisiana State Univ. Press, 2003), 4. See also James M. McPherson, "The War That Never Goes Away," in *Drawn with the Sword: Reflections on the American Civil War* (New York: Oxford University Press, 1996), 55–66.

11. Prior to the recent wave of scholarship, the Civil War was all but ignored by academic historians. As Edward Ayers has observed, "The war itself became something of a schol-

arly backwater, neglected by the leading historians of nineteenth century America. The distaste for the war in Vietnam manifested itself in an aversion to any kind of military history, while the fascination with social history made generals and their maneuvers seem irrelevant and boring at best." Edward Ayers, "Worrying about the Civil War," in *Moral Problems in American Life: New Perspectives on Cultural History*, eds. Karen Halttunen and Lewis Perry (Ithaca: Cornell University Press, 1998), 155.

12. Email from James M. McPherson to Drew Faust, October 7, 2003.
13. Toplin, "Introduction," in *Ken Burns's The Civil War*, xv; Burns, "Four O'Clock in the Morning Courage," ibid., 164.
14. Adam I. P. Smith and Peter J. Parish, "A Contested Legacy: The Civil War and Party Politics in the North," in *Legacy of Disunion*, eds. Grant and Parish, 81; David Montgomery, *The American Civil War and the Meanings of Freedom* (New York: Oxford University Press, 1987), 1. See also Robert Penn Warren, *The Legacy of the Civil War: Meditations on the Centennial* (New York: Random House, 1961).
15. Gabor Boritt, "Lincoln and Gettysburg," in *Ken Burns's The Civil War*, ed. Toplin, 84. Boritt cites his own phone discussions with Powell in 1992 as well as newspaper reports. Boritt has also pointed out to me that the creation of the Lincoln Prize in 1991, with its $50,000 award for a work of Civil War scholarship, may have helped attract historians' attention to the war.
16. James M. McPherson and William J. Cooper Jr., eds., *Writing the Civil War: The Quest to Understand* (Columbia: University of South Carolina Press, 1998), 3; Maris A. Vinovskis, ed., *Toward a Social History of the American Civil War: Exploratory Essays* (New York: Cambridge University Press, 1990). See also McPherson, *Drawn with the Sword*.
17. This is from the mission statement for the Great Campaigns of the Civil War Series at the University of Nebraska Press, Brooks Simpson and Anne Bailey, series editors.
18. James M. McPherson, *For Cause and Comrades: Why Men Fought in the Civil War* (New York: Oxford University Press, 1997), x; Hemingway quoted by David Lipsky in "Left Behind," *New York Times Book Review*, December 14, 2003, 9. See also Emory Thomas, "Rebellion and Conventional Warfare," in *Writing the Civil War*, 59.
19. Mark Grimsley, reviews of *This Terrible Sword*, by Peter Cozzens, and *Pea Ridge* by William Shea and Earl J. Hess, *Journal of Southern History* 60 (May 1994): 405.
20. For examples of these interpretations see Paul D. Escott, *Many Excellent People: Power and Privilege in North Carolina, 1850–1900* (Chapel Hill: University of North Carolina Press, 1985); J. Tracy Power, *Lee's Miserables* (Chapel Hill: University of North Carolina Press, 1998); Earl J. Hess, *The Union Soldier in Battle* (Lawrence: University of Kansas Press, 1997); Reid Mitchell, *Civil War Soldiers* (New York: Viking, 1998); *The Civil War Soldier: A Historical Reader*, eds. Michael Barton and Larry M. Logue (New York: New York University Press, 2002); Drew Gilpin Faust, "Altars of Sacrifice: Confederate Women and the Narratives of War," *Journal of American History* 76 (March 1990): 1200–28; Elizabeth D. Leonard, *All the Daring of the Soldier: Women of the Civil War Armies* (New York: Norton, 1999); Deanne Blanton and Lauren M. Cook, *They Fought Like Demons: Women Soldiers in the American Civil War* (Baton Rouge: Louisiana State University Press, 2002); Barbara J. Fields, "Who Freed the Slaves?" in Geoffrey Ward, *The Civil War* (New York: Alfred Knopf, 1990), 178–79; Ira Berlin, "Emancipation and Its Meaning in American Life," *Reconstruction* 2 (1994).
21. Toplin, quoting Burns in "Introduction," Toplin, ed., *Ken Burns's The Civil War*, xxii.
22. McPherson, *Drawn with the Sword*, 57; "Brady's Photographs of the War," *New York Times*, Sept. 26, 1862, and "Pictures of the Dead at Antietam," *New York Times*, Oct. 20, 1862. See Geoffrey Gorer, "The Pornography of Death," *Encounter* 5 (1955): 49–52.
23. Chris Hedges, *War Is a Force That Gives Us Meaning* (New York: Public Affairs Press, 2002). As novelist and literary critic Nancy Huston has written, "Specifically in order

that human violence not be reducible to animal violence, it is imperative for men to establish a narrative sequence." By its very definition as war, violence gains a logic, a structure, a goal, *a story*. Nancy Huston, "Tales of War and Tears of Women," *Women's Studies International Forum* 5 (1982): 271. See also Margaret Mead, "Warfare Is Only an Invention—Not a Biological Necessity," *Asia* 40 (1940): 402–5.

24. Hedges, *War Is a Force*, 91; Susan Sontag, *Regarding the Pain of Others* (New York: Farrar, Straus, Giroux, 2003), 122. See also a powerful statement on the attractions of war: James Carroll, "War's Power of Seduction," *Boston Globe*, Mar. 11, 2003.
25. George Mosse, quoted in David Maraniss, *They Marched into Sunlight* (New York: Simon and Schuster, 2003), 101.
26. Michael Herr, *Dispatches* (1977; rpt, New York: Avon Books, 1978), 260–61.
27. I refer here, of course, to Daniel Aaron, *The Unwritten War: American Writers and the Civil War* (New York: Knopf, 1973).
28. Faust, "Altars of Sacrifice."

CHAPTER 11

1. Kris Rampersad, *Finding a Place: Indo Trinidadian Literature* (Kingston, Jamaica: Ian Randle, 2002), 39, 50, 52.
2. Ibid., 69.
3. Derek Walcott, *The Antilles: Fragments of Epic Memory (The Nobel Lecture)* (New York: Farrar, Straus and Giroux, 1993), 7.
4. Nadine Gordimer, "The Essential Gesture," *Granta* 15 (1985): 137–51.
5. Rampersad, *Finding a Place*, 69.

CHAPTER 13

1. I have altered this person's name to protect his identity.
2. Harold Lasswell, *Politics: Who Gets What, When, How* (New York: McGraw-Hill, 1936).
3. National Research Council, *Review of New York State Low-Level Radioactive Waste Siting Process.* (Washington, D.C.: National Academy Press, 1996).
4. Doug McAdam, Sidney Tarrow, and Charles Tilly, *Dynamics of Contention* (New York: Cambridge University Press, 2001).

CONTRIBUTORS

Jodi Bromberg received her juris doctorate from Temple University in May 2005 and a B.A. from the University of Pennsylvania. She is currently a litigation associate at a Philadelphia law firm. In addition, she writes *The 3L Word* (www.the3lword.blogspot.com), a blog about political, social, and legal issues.

Catherine Clinton is the author and editor of more than twenty books, including *The Plantation Mistress*, *Tara Revisted*, and, most recently, *Harriet Tubman: The Road to Freedom*. She has written books for children including *A Poem of Her Own* and, most recently, *Hold The Flag High*. She is currently researching a biography of Mary Todd Lincoln, and completing a piece, "Sexual Hypocrisy from Thomas Jefferson to Strom Thurmond," for the Feminist Sexual Ethics Project volume *Slavery's Long Shadow*.

Caitlin Love Crowell is a doctoral candidate in history at Yale University. She has a B.A. from the women's studies program at the University at Buffalo and an M.A. in history from the University of South Florida. Her dissertation explores the intimate lives of black women activists in the late nineteenth and twentieth centuries, insisting on the importance of the personal stories of public figures. She dedicates her article to the memory of the Shanton sisters.

John D'Emilio teaches gender studies and history at the University of Illinois–Chicago, and was the founding director of the Policy Institute of the National Gay and Lesbian Task Force. His books include *Sexual Politics, Sexual Communities: The Making of a Homosexual Minority in the United States* and *Lost Prophet: The Life and Times of Bayard Rustin*.

Jim Downs earned his B.A. from the University of Pennsylvania and his M.A. and Ph.D. from Columbia University. He is the coeditor of *Taking Back the Academy: History of Activism, History as Activism*. He is currently a lecturer in the history department at Princeton University.

Jennifer Fronc is an assistant professor of social and women's history at Virginia Commonwealth University. She earned her Ph.D. in history at Columbia University in 2005.

Drew Gilpin Faust is the Lincoln Professor of History and dean of the Radcliff Institute for Advanced Study at Harvard University. Her publications include *Mothers of Invention: Women of the Slaveholding South in the American Civil War*; *Southern Stories: Slaveholders in Peace and War*; *James Henry Hammond and the Old South: A Design for Mastery*; *The Creation of Confederate Nationalism: Ideology and Identity in the Civil War South*; and *A Sacred Circle: The Dilemma of the Intellectual in the Old South*.

Jill Lepore is a professor of history at Harvard University and the author of *New York Burning: Liberty, Slavery, and Conspiracy in Eighteenth-Century Manhattan*; *A is for American: Letters and Other Characters in the Newly United States*; and *The Name of War: King Philip's War and the Origins of American Identity*, which was a winner of the Bancroft Prize. She is cofounder of the online history magazine *Common-place* (www.common-place.org).

Erme C. Maula is an advanced-practice community health nurse who strives for social justice. She is a consultant for the Philadelphia Department of Public Health coordinating HIV/AIDS programs and ensuring that people have access to appropriate health care. On a regional and national level she is a vocal advocate for the visibility of Asian and Pacific Islander communities as the chair of both the East Coast Asian AIDS Network and the Asian and Pacific Islander Women's HIV/AIDS National Network.

Timothy Patrick McCarthy is a lecturer on history and literature and on women, gender, and sexuality at Harvard University. An award-winning teacher and activist, he is also coeditor, with John McMillian, of *The Radical Reader: A Documentary Anthology of the American Radical Tradition* and, with John Stauffer, of *Prophets of Protest: Reconsidering* *the History of American Abolitionism.* He is currently working on a book about African-American church burnings in the American South.

Jennifer Morgan is an associate professor of history and women's and gender studies at Rutgers University. She is the author of *Laboring Women: Reproduction and Gender in New World Slavery* and is currently working on a study of demography and numeracy in early American slave societies.

Eleanor M. Novek has a Ph.D. from the University of Pennsylvania and is an associate professor in the Department of Communication at Monmouth University in West Long Branch, New Jersey, where she teaches journalism and is director of the graduate program in corporate and public communication. A former newspaper reporter and editor, her research interests include communication for social justice and the use of journalistic practice as a strategy for empowerment (currently in the context of a women's prison). She has published a number of book chapters and articles in the *Journalism, Communication Studies, Discourse and Society,* the *Howard Journal of Communications,* the *Atlantic Journal of Communication, Women's Studies in Communication,* and other peer-reviewed journals. She has received grants from the American Association of University Women and the Freedom Forum and fellowships from the Poynter Institute for Media Studies, the Spencer Foundation, and the Annenberg School for Communication at the University of Pennsylvania.

Jung H. Pak earned her B.A. from Colgate University and is currently completing her Ph.D. in U.S. history at Columbia University. She was a Fulbright Scholar for 2003–2004.

Sasha Kamini Parmasad was born and raised in Trinidad and Tobago and lived as a child in New Delhi, India, between 1988 and 1992. She received her B.A. in English literature and studio art at Williams College in 2002. She is currently enrolled in the creative writing program at Columbia University, where she is also an instructor in the undergraduate writing program, and was an instructor in the creative writing summer program for high school students in 2003. Her first novel, *Ink and Sugar,* a work in progress, won third place in the long fiction category in the First Words South Asian Literary Contest in 2003. Her poetry is forthcoming in the anthology of South Asian-American poetry *Writing the Lines of Our Hands.*

Rebecca Sanford has a Ph.D. from Temple University. She is an Assistant Professor at Monmouth University, where she teaches in the interpersonal theory and family communication areas. Her research interests include interpersonal communication aspects of relationship formation and maintenance, especially in under-researched relationships such as friendship. She is a coauthor of the forthcoming *Interpersonal Communication across the Lifespan* textbook.

Daniel J. Sherman has a Ph.D. in government from Cornell University. He is currently the Luce-Funded Professor of Environmental Policy and Decision Making at the University of Puget Sound in Tacoma, Washington. His work on local environmental movements in the United States is supported by the Heinz Foundation, the Morris K. Udall Foundation, and the National Science Foundation.

Index

A

Abolitionists, 37, 93
Academia, 18, 25, 44, 160
    culture of, 20
    responsibilities of, 148
Academic curiosity, 158
Academic publication, 156
Academic relevance, 149
Access, request for, 151
Acclaim, 24
Accountability, 25
Activism, 41, 160, 162
Activists, nurses as, 159
Advocacy, 160
Advocate, 14
Affirmation, prison writing and, 118
African-American studies, 22, 35, 42
    Civil War, 102
African-American women, 42, 69
Age, issues of in Korea, 58
Ain't I am Woman?, 41
Alcohol addiction, among the incarcerated
    populations, 112
Alexander Hamilton, 83
Amazon Quarterly, 14
"America Made Easy," 83
American conservatism, 58
American cultural imperialism, 128
American Dream, 29
American elite, 29, 32
American foreign policy, 51
American Heritage, 84
American Historical Association, 84
American Historical Review, 99
American Slavery, American Freedom, 43
American Social Science Association, 84

American Studies Association of Korea
    (ASAK), 58
Analysis, burden of, 162
Antietam, 97, 105
Antiquarianism, 89
Antiracism, 42
Antislavery movement, 93
Anzaldúa, Gloria, 41
Apartheid, 128
Archives, 40, 43
Ar'n't I a Woman?, 41
Articulation of self, 129
Asian families, stresses on, 165
Asian and Pacific Islander women, HIV/AIDS
    movement and, 162, 165
Assertion of self, 129
Assumptions, 166
Audience
    relationship of writers to, 122
    responsibilities of writers to, 19
Awards, 24

B

Baby activists, 42
Baldwin, James, 27
Battle Cry of Freedom, 99; *see also* McPherson,
    James
Beard, Charles and Mary, 30
Beaver, R. Pierce, 51
Bechloss, Michael, 83
Bell, Derrick, 146
Bender, Thomas, 60
    *Rethinking American History in a Global
        Age*, 53
Benjamin, Judah P., 96

effect of television on, 132
Indians in Trinidad, 129
Cultural taboos, 167
Cultural understanding, 56
Cultural warriors, 34
Culture, 35, 72

D

Davis, Angela, 166
Davis, Natalie, 19, 86
Death, cultural taboos around, 168
Debates, 15
DeBow's Review, 96
Declaration of Independence, 29
Defamation, 144
D'Emilio, John, 14, 15
Democracy, 16, 50
Demos, John, 86
Descriptive narratives, 85
Desegregation, 140
    laws of, 146
Discourse, history of, 67
Discrimination, 128, 141
    lesbian, gay, bisexual, and transgender,
        144
Disempowerment, 144
Disenfranchisement, 144
Disorientation, 54
Dispatches, 107
Dissemblance, 72
Diversity, 26
Divestment, 42
Divine purification, war as a process of, 96
Doctoral theses, 18, 44, 61, 160
Dostoyevsky, Fyodor, 79
Douglass, Frederick, 37
Douglass, Helen, 74
Drug addiction, among the incarcerated
    populations, 112
Duke University, 42
Dunning, William Archibald, 30

E

Early American history, 43
Economic justice, 16, 157
Editing, effect of on self-image of women
    prisoners, 120
Educational disadvantage, among the
    incarcerated populations, 112

Educational paralysis, 167
Education programs in prisons, 119
Elements of Style, 44
Ellison, Ralph, 35
Emancipation, 73
Embodiment, 40
Emotion, issues of, 72, 75
Empowerment, prison writing as a
        source of, 121
Endurance, 128
Enlightenment theories, 93
Enslavement, 39
Enthrallment, 90
Enthusiasm, 26
Environmental justice, 150, 153
    issues relating to, 157
Environmental policies, 148
Environmental studies, politics of, 147
Ethnicity, issues of in Korea, 58
Exhaustion as a barrier to writing, 161

F

Fag Rag, 14
Fame, prison writing as a source of, 121
Family Health Project, 163
Family relationships, preservation of for
        imprisoned women, 117
Family values, 58
Feelings, 132
Female inmates. *See also* Incarcerated women
    effect of editing on self-image of, 120
    writing topics of, 116
Female sexual desire, 64
Feminism, 15
    sex debates of, 65
Feminist history, 72
Feminist research, 111
Fieldwork, conducting, 148
Finances, 164
Fischer, David Hackett, 83
Fitzgerald, F. Scott, 103
Folk poems, 127
Forced sexual encounters, 61, 63, 67
Foreign policy, American, 51
Forten, Charlotte, 74
Forten, Francis, 74
Fortune, prison writing as a source of, 121
Foucault, Michel, 112
Franklin, Jon, 87
Freedman, Estelle, 15

CPSIA information can be obtained
at www.ICGtesting.com
Printed in the USA
LVHW021158210822
726458LV00007B/141